LUTHERANS
in CONCERT

The Story of the National Lutheran Council, 1918-1966

Frederick K. Wentz

AUGSBURG PUBLISHING HOUSE
MINNEAPOLIS, MINNESOTA

LUTHERANS IN CONCERT

Copyright © 1968 Augsburg Publishing House

Library of Congress Catalog Card No. 68-13727

MANUFACTURED IN THE UNITED STATES OF AMERICA

Preface

In the latter years of the National Lutheran Council one of its executives, reviewing a document which crossed his desk, changed the phrase "cooperative Lutheranism" to "cooperative Lutheran activities." He was reflecting a policy of his organization, determined by the Lutheran denominations it served, namely, that the National Lutheran Council was simply and purely the agency for carrying through certain activities of the church bodies themselves. Unconsciously, however, this executive and his policy were denying that "cooperative Lutheranism" was a reality in itself, a thing of substance in history, a movement.

Yet the first thing the historian wants to say about twentieth century American inter-Lutheran cooperation is that it is a significant historical movement. Any historical movement has its own particular spirit and its own peculiar course of events. Any such movement finds embodiment in certain leaders and characteristic activities. It takes its shape by the way many people respond to the challenges of its leaders and are caught up in its activities. This description fits "cooperative Lutheranism" in twentieth century America. Until 1967 the central organization of this movement was the National Lutheran Council.

The purpose of this volume is to describe that movement (until it entered a new phase in 1967) with special reference to the National Lutheran Council.

Of course, like any historical movement, cooperative Lutheranism had its taut inner tensions. There was, for example, the question about the mandate and power of the people who became NLC staff. Were they given freedom for pioneering and prophetic leadership, or were they simply to carry out duties painstakingly defined by the denominational leaders who made up their board of directors and carefully circumscribed by the decisions of national conventions of Lutheran bodies? This was an unresolved issue from the time European Commissioner John A. Morehead gave unauthorized kinds of help to European churches after World War I to the last years when official policy rejected the very concept of cooperative Lutheranism. Inevitably the trend was toward a more timid, frictionless pattern. At the same time, many of the pioneer steps in any decade became in later decades the routine functions of both National Lutheran Council and its member churches.

In tracing the story of a movement one can best start by describing its contexts or settings, then detailing its organizational life—programs, ideas, growth, personalities, trends, ending with some overall assessment of the movement's inner spirit, its historical impact, its major significance for theology and church history. That will be the sequence for this volume.

If, as we are suggesting, cooperative Lutheranism in twentieth century America is to be viewed as an entity in itself, one would have to set it off from other movements and events, stressing discontinuities and making these other events simply the backdrop or the context for the story. There is a historical context, events leading up to the movement, and there is the contemporary setting, parallel and intersecting phenomena during the same decades.

These two contexts could just as readily be described as continuities, emphasizing that cooperative Lutheranism is one piece with many other movements in the stream of history. Then one would speak of lineal (historical) continuities and lateral (contemporary) continuities. Either perspective—seeing simply contexts or seeing continuities—is true; cooperative Lutheranism is both a movement in itself and an integral part of larger trends and events. This volume will focus on the former perspective without losing sight of the latter.

Many people have assisted in the preparing of this volume. I want particularly to recognize Miss Helen M. Knubel, whose personal helpfulness, enthusiasm, and knowledge have been an invaluable aid during the thirteen months I served as "Archivist Consultant" for the National Lutheran Council and during the writing of these pages. She has prepared the bibliography, the lists of names at the end of the book, and the selection of pictures. Careful readings of the manuscript by Paul C. Empie and Abdel Ross Wentz have proved quite helpful.

FREDERICK K. WENTZ

September 1, 1967

Contents

Refugees
CYCOM
Fine Middle-Aged Fettle

Latin America
Division of LWF Affairs
Urban Church Planning
Other American Missions Work
Radio and Television
Movie-Making
Public Relations
Welfare Gains
Immigrant Services
Changes in Campus Ministry
Services to Military Personnel
Large, Broad, Diversified

Search for New Cooperative Patterns
Formation of LCUSA
Age of Dialogue
Exchange Programs
Theological Dialogues
An Altered International Outreach
A Voice in National Policies
Immigration Legislation
Lively Seeds

Taking Stock
Slow but Steady Progress
Unity, Identity, Mission
The Conciliar Movement

Picture Section: 16-page insert following page 118

INTRODUCTION | Contexts for Cooperation

Contemporary Scene

Coming into existence in 1918, the National Lutheran Council emerged at a significant hinge-point in the history of western civilization and in the history of its churches. To be sure, one of the most pervasive forces shaping the twentieth century—the rise of technology—had been at work for many decades and was simply hurling itself upon the twentieth century with impacted force because of its geometric progression, throwing us into one tight world that is complexly interrelated. But three events in the second decade of the century point to major shifts in western history.

One of these events was World War I (1914-1918), which can be viewed as the beginning of a time of troubles (wars, depressions, dictators, revolutions) that has not ended. The relative peace and complacency of nineteenth century European culture were shattered. Much of Europe was devastated; its self-confidence was shaken. The destruction of cities and the widespread disruption of peoples and economies, together with the hatreds and carnage of war itself, produced misery and cynicism in Europe, shock and sympathy in America. For Lutherans the war, coupled with the virtual closing of immigration into the United States in 1924, meant a sudden reversal of roles for Europeans and Americans. Scattered Lutheran immigrants, psychologically children of Europe, became suddenly the wealthy relatives with resources to help the unfortunates of Europe. This is an exaggeration of the facts, but it is hardly an exaggeration of the psychological impact of the decade following 1915 upon America's Lutherans.

In a broader, less tangible way, the coming of the Bolsheviks in Russia in 1917 has had a still greater impact on twentieth century civilization and church life. Distinctly hostile to Christianity, Communism has come to encompass one-third of the globe and has political and ideological potency at many other places. The Bolsheviks in 1917 signaled the end of the concept of Christendom—the idea that a certain territory, mainly Europe and its colonies, with its culture, institutions, people, and ideas belonged to the Christian faith. For Lutherans Nazism in Germany in the 1930's provided a second and convincing evidence that the idea of Christendom no longer had meaning.

Of course, this idea had been dying for a long time. The process can be called secularization. For centuries philosophy, economic life, the arts and sciences had been spinning off into separate worlds of thought and action without reference to theology or control by the authoritative institutions of church and state. But in the twentieth century not only has secularism gone global and become all-pervasive; it also has spawned explosive social movements that thrive on irrational communal passions and elevate social and ideological goals to the level of religious commitment. Today, when populations and the social structures are much larger, men seek to merge their identities in great collectivities. It is the Collective Age, and many of the movements of the day are utterly indifferent to Christianity or are actively hostile toward it. Similarly, it is the Pluralist Age in which men and nations of radically differing world-views stand cheek to jowl on a shrinking planet, rattling increasingly threatening weapons at each other, yet entering into serious dialogue in a desperate effort to find some common bases for mutual understanding and peaceful coexistence.

The history of the churches has taken an equally sharp turn into the twentieth century. Just a few years before the coming of World War and Bolsheviks, in 1910, was held the great world missionary conference at Edinburgh which symbolized the opening of the Ecumenical Era in church history. Now the many churches scattered throughout the world have become sharply aware of each other, acutely conscious of their corporate unity in Christ despite many barriers and differences, and newly cognizant of the burning mission which Christians together are to carry to the whole modern world. In our day the church has become a world-wide fellowship and, at the same time, a self-conscious minority newly aware of other religious blocs and the social movements that by-pass all traditional religions. At many places Christianity has received harsh treatment; it is pruning time for the churches. On the other hand, Christians have rediscovered the church herself, her real nature and her true mission. It is the Ecumenical Era.

Historical Background

To understand a movement toward cooperative Lutheranism by twentieth century Americans one must bear in mind the contemporary setting as it has just been sketched. Equally important is the context from which the new trends emerged, that is, the historical background.

From 1750 to 1914, as secularism advanced, western civilization was left without any strong integrating force. Its authoritative institutions were losing their power. It was the day of liberalism and individualism, of political democracy and economic laissez-faire, of increasing religious tolerance. Indeed it was a time of *atomization*—many nations, each trying to act independently, and many individuals, men who considered themselves self-made, free-standing, not embedded in kinship or social institutions, each an independent unit. It was the era of private life under Jefferson's ideal of each family living peaceably on its own small farm.

Church life took the shape of the age. It was a period of growth for the free churches, in which adult Christians came together and covenanted under God to make a congregation. For most laymen the local congregation pretty well represented their picture of the church. Various denominations grew up as free associations of Christians who had common objectives. In America even people of state-church background got used to the voluntary system and counted churchmanship in terms of their gifts and their congregational activities. Typically, especially in the American nations, men no longer viewed the church as their mother who had nurtured them but rather as their daughter for whose care they must take responsibility.

Preeminently it was the Age of Evangelicalism. Evangelicalism makes central the believer's personal experience of Jesus Christ. It lays stress upon "heart religion," conversion, personal and enthusiastic loyalty to Jesus Christ, growth in holiness, missionary zeal, and the practical consequences in one's personal habits of life. Identified first with the pietism of Philip Jacob Spener in Germany and the Wesleyan movement in Britain, it found characteristic expression in the great tides of revivals which have typified American Christianity for two centuries and had parallel surges among British and continental Protestants. It was, by and large, a kind of Christianity which underplayed the role of tradition and the Christian heritage, except the Bible itself, which had little feel for the organic or organizational unity of the church, and which failed to relate the faith effectively to the social structures of political and economic life.

American Lutheranism, shaped during this period, reflected all the characteristics enumerated—individualism, congregationalism, denominationalism, and pietism. In the eighteenth century it was German pietism that marked the spirit of the scattered Lutherans on this continent. In the nineteenth century pietism continued to be strong. But a movement toward stricter adherence to the Lutheran confessions, greatly strengthened by a continuing stream of more orthodox Lutheran groups from Europe, added to American Lutheranism as a whole a cast of rigid orthodoxy that distinguished it sharply from the surrounding Protestantism as well as from much of world Lutheranism.

Furthermore, differing degrees of orthodoxy provided points of controversy which helped to keep Lutherans separated from each other on this continent, without ties of fellowship or the loosest of organizational structures that could represent more than a small fraction of the total membership.

From the earliest days of colonial America Lutherans had been separated from each other by the differences of national background, of language, of type of piety, and by the historical accident of widely separated settlement in the new land. It is true that during the three decades following 1820 a loose national confederation, the General Synod, provided a rallying point for a sizeable percentage of America's Lutherans by uniting as many regional bodies or synods as it could attract. But the newer immigrants held aloof, considering the General Synod too American- ized and too relaxed in its confessional subscription. Then in the decades following 1850 the General Synod itself was splintered by controversy and by regional withdrawal. Meanwhile the newcomers from Scandinavia and Germany formed numerous synods and reached out for larger fellowship. They too, however, fell into theological controversy and made only limited progress in inter-Lutheran fellowship.

In the decades from 1880 to 1918 the bitterness of theological conflict abated and the suspicion and sectarian distrust among American Lutherans were relaxed to a notable degree. A conservative confessionalism was dominant in all major groups. Outright attacks upon each other became rare, yet differences were keenly felt and an atmosphere of distrust remained.

At the turn of the century certain factors were helping to dispel the distrust, and certain actions pointed to the possibilities that lay in cooperation. These events belong to the story of the beginnings of the movement for cooperative Lutheranism in twentieth century America.

I

Prelude and Beginnings

⊢ Early in the 1900's there were twenty-one separate Lutheran church bodies in America with eighteen different languages spoken in their congregations. Though the sharpest theological controversies were past, the leaders of these bodies viewed each other with suspicion, and the members lived in isolation from their counterparts in other Lutheran churches. The Lutheran people were mostly rural and immigrant, psychologically isolated, living in their hyphenated shells (as Norwegian-Americans, German-Americans, Swedish-Americans, etc.), defensive of their Lutheran and ethnic heritage. Their clergymen, though divided among themselves in interpretation of the confessions, were uniformly nurtured on the theology of seventeenth century scholastic orthodoxy, which was defended militantly in many of the church bodies as the one correct pattern of God's truth revealed through Christ in Scripture.

However, at the dawn of the century there were harbingers of change. Lutherans were prospering. Lutheran churches were growing rather steadily in size and number. Lutherans had their share in the movement to the cities where neighbors were very different and where there were stimulating new intellectual currents. Auxiliaries and other additions to congregational life had significant beginnings in the early 1900's. The slow increase of paid synodical officials anticipated the church bureaucracies of the late twentieth century, just as improved methods of money-raising—stewardship and benevolence programs—started to find their way into church life.

Three Mergers

After 1910 several Lutheran church merger negotiations began to move, three of them coming to fruition near the time of the birth of the National Lutheran Council. Each was limited to a particular national background or the reunion of bodies that had broken apart in the nineteenth century. One of these, the formation in 1919 of the body called the Wisconsin Synod, brought together conservative Lutherans who have never had any part in the National Lutheran Council. For four decades the Wisconsin Synod participated in the Synodical Conference, a loose fellowship of Lutheran bodies, the largest of which was the Lutheran Church—Missouri Synod. Founded in 1872, the Synodical Conference maintained that cooperation among Lutherans awaits complete accord in doctrine and in controverted practices.

The other two mergers were important factors in the formation of the National Lutheran Council. The first of these brought into one body the great majority of the Norwegian-American Lutherans. Though sharply divided in type of piety and often at odds theologically, the Norwegian bodies that emerged in nineteenth century America persisted in seeking union among themselves. In 1890 three of them succeeded in forming the United Norwegian Lutheran Church in America, which in June of 1917 joined with the Norwegian Synod and Hauge's Synod to form the Norwegian Lutheran Church of America (changed in title in 1946 to the Evangelical Lutheran Church). First president of this new body was H. G. Stub, who became the first president of the National Lutheran Council the following year.

The other merger, consummated in November 1918, just two months after the National Lutheran Council came into being, constituted the largest of the Lutheran church bodies with a confirmed membership of nearly 800,000—the United Lutheran Church in America. At the time of the Civil War two major groups which broke with the General Synod had created their own general bodies. They were the southerners who formed what became the United Synod of the South, and a more conservative group which became the General Council, advocating a more complete subscription to the historic confessions. It was these three bodies, with their common base in the eastern part of the United States and their common origins in colonial history, that reunited in 1918. Theological differences had virtually disappeared as the General Synod had grown steadily more conservative. Over several decades there were exchanges of fraternal delegates, free conferences across synodical lines, the development of a common liturgy and hymnbook, cooperation in foreign missions, and a number of other informal associations that combined people of the three synods. It became obvious that organic union was in the offing. The planning and the enthusiasm for the four hundredth anniversary of the Reformation in 1917 provided the occasion for specific proposals and completion of the union. The United Lutheran Church in America was the largest and one of the most active elements in the life of the National Lutheran Council. It was by conviction committed from the start to cooperation among the various Lutheran bodies.

Reformation Quadricentennial

The same planning and enthusiasm for the Reformation celebration of 1917 were also a major factor leading to the emergence of the National Lutheran Council itself. Here was a nationwide interest in the great events and principles of the sixteenth century which were a precious heritage held in common by all Lutherans. In cities and towns across the country committees were formed, including different branches of Lutheranism; in many cases they were working together for the very first time.

Two of these inter-Lutheran groups planning for the Quadricentennial gained nationwide prominence. One of them, called for as early as 1909 by the General Council, brought representatives of the General Council, the General Synod, and the United Synod South into a committee which first met in 1914. It set up offices in Philadelphia with the Reverend Howard R. Gold as its executive. It prepared appropriate literature and a commemorative medal, promoted lectures and sermons and articles, and provided for great joint celebrations in cities across the land.

The other planning committee was created by the Lutheran Society of New York, a society of several hundred Lutheran laymen who belonged to the six Lutheran bodies represented in the New York City area. Guiding spirit for this Reformation Quadricentenary Committee was the Reverend William S. Schoenfeld and the director was the Reverend Otto H. Pannkoke, both Missouri Synod pastors, the latter also a graduate student in history with an interest in public relations. This committee took a broader approach in seeking to promote civic celebrations that would recognize the contribution of the Reformation to ongoing civilization. It prepared speakers' booklets, a *Bulletin,* and a variety of literature. The committee had signal success, for Lutherans of that day, in attracting the attention of great universities, securing space in the nation's daily newspapers, and involving nationally known leaders in its main events.

Following the celebrations the latter committee reorganized itself in November 1917 on a permanent basis as the Lutheran Bureau, continuing O. H. Pannkoke as its director. It was to be an independent agency of publicity for the Lutheran churches of the nation. Within the year Pannkoke was agitating for a national Lutheran council and his bureau soon became an organ of that infant organization.

World War

Meanwhile, in April of 1917, the United States entered the World War as the enemy of Germany. Like all American citizens the Lutherans were profoundly affected by this turn of events. Most German Lutherans had been sympathetic to the cause of Germany in the war. Now they felt torn in their sympathies, though the vast majority of them quickly affirmed their loyalty to the United States government and its purposes in going to war. Nonetheless, the sudden surge of an emotional patriotism among the citizenry turned suspicion toward all foreign-language groups, so that Lutherans as individuals and as a religious group suffered much ill will and some outright persecution. At the same time training camps for troops and the increased war effort created emergency needs for the ministrations of the churches.

To bring spiritual assistance to the boys in military service Lutheran laymen created an organization that soon had 60,000 men enrolled as supporters. By November of 1917 a more permanent organization emerged, the Lutheran Brotherhood of America. Its function became largely that of erecting and equipping buildings near camp sites.

Several other Lutheran efforts at war work sprang up. During the summer of 1917 steps were taken to coordinate these in order to eliminate confusion and overlapping programs and in order to give Lutheranism a united representation before the government in this emergency situation. Thus there was created the Lutheran Commission for Soldiers' and Sailors' Welfare on October 19, 1917. It was a remarkable organization which only dire emergency could have effected, since it represented all Lutheran bodies except those of the Synodical Conference. The Conference, which organized its own Army and Navy Board, cooperated with the Commission at a number of points, an equally precedent-breaking development.

Immediately the Commission set out to raise an ambitious three quarters of a million dollars in a few months. Walton H. Greever of South Carolina, editor of the *American Lutheran Survey,* came to New York to direct the nationwide campaign. All the facilities of the Lutheran Bureau were enlisted. A speakers' manual was prepared. A meeting for national strategy and leader-training was held. Church officials were mobilized to give their support. Pastors and church papers were supplied with information. About a quarter of a million pieces of literature were mailed from the central office in three weeks. By the middle of February Lutherans across the nation had responded enthusiastically with $1,350,000. It was an unprecedented inter-Lutheran campaign and financial response, an exhilarating experience for Lutheran leaders.

The Commission's activities were carried through with equal enthusiasm and dedication. Its main thrust was providing pastoral services at training camps. With the Lutheran Brotherhood erecting facilities, more than thirty centers were staffed with Lutheran pastors. More than a hundred other men were sent to camps as spiritual counselors and supported in their work by traveling field secretaries. The Commission also chose Lutheran chaplains for the army and the navy and provided them with suitable literature.

A variety of related tasks were carried through by the Commission. A women's committee enlisted volunteers to knit thousands of garments for soldiers. Service houses were maintained in four eastern cities and many special services were performed for military men and their families. Worship was conducted for interned aliens in Georgia and Utah. A ministry to soldiers and sailors in hospitals was undertaken.

One primary reason for creation of the Commission was to provide Lutherans with united representation before the national government. For this purpose an office was maintained at Washington with the Reverend Lauritz Larsen in charge. When the Commission sought to send its workers to France, following the troops, the War Department refused, wanting the YMCA to handle all overseas Protestant work. By persisting the Lutherans were finally able to send representatives to investigate the needs in France. Carrying this responsibility were the Reverend Charles J. Smith and the Honorable Frank M. Riter, to be followed later by the Reverend M. J. Stolee. These contacts in France, though of only marginal significance in the Commission's work, proved to be important beginnings for renewed American Lutheran relations with European Lutheranism.

Officers of the wartime Commission included Lauritz Larsen as secretary and the Honorable E. F. Eilert as treasurer. The Reverend J. A. O. Stub served as executive secretary.

Chairman of the Commission until its demise in 1922 was a Manhattan pastor and representative of the General Synod, Frederick H. Knubel. In 1918 Dr. Knubel became the first president of the United Lutheran Church in America, a position he served with distinction for twenty-six years. Dr. Knubel brought rare talents of dedicated leadership to his many responsibilities in the Lutheran church. He was both wise and firm in his principles, yet diplomatic in his ability to bring diverse viewpoints into cooperation, a man to inspire confidence. He also combined a spiritual depth with direct executive ability. His leadership was one important factor in the success of the Commission as an unprecedented step in inter-Lutheran cooperation.

From this emergency Commission there came, in less than a year's time, a permanent inter-Lutheran cooperative agency, the National Lutheran Council. The constituting action was taken by the presidents of the participating Lutheran bodies but the initiative was supplied by the wartime Commission with Frederick Knubel and Lauritz Larsen as its representatives in this undertaking. In 1919 Larsen asserted concerning the new Council that Knubel was "the one man who exerted the greatest influence toward its formation." [1]

To be sure, there was a general sense of urgency and of inter-Lutheran goodwill. And there were other suggestions of a common agency. As early as 1915 a meeting in Toledo, Ohio, called by C. H. L. Schuette, the President of the Joint Synod of Ohio, had prepared a constitution for a federation of Lutheran Churches in America. And on June 27, 1918, the National Lutheran Editors' Association in its Chicago convention passed a resolution looking toward a common agency.[2] The Lutheran Bureau was also interested in this development.

But it was the immediate experience of the Soldiers' and Sailors' Commission which provoked action. Its success in getting Lutherans to do a big job together made obvious the benefits of practical cooperation. In fact, its operations made clear to many Lutherans the necessity of a common agency for the efficient functioning of the church. Yet the Commission was constituted as an emergency measure with carefully circumscribed duties. It received requests for broader actions which it could not take. Even as the war ended (November 1918) it became involved in services—a ministry to industrial workers in impacted areas— which promised to be long-range undertakings. Furthermore, Lutheran statesmen could see that there would be continued urgent need for a united Lutheran voice vis-à-vis the government, for united Lutheran campaigns for funds and publicity, and for united action in future disasters in America as well as the now looming emergency needs of European brethren. Thus the Commission began to plan for a permanent agency to take over and to expand its functions.

Three Pressing Needs

Three needs for concerted action were most pressing and were widely recognized in Lutheran circles as compelling problems.

The first of these was called the language question. It was the need for vigorous action to defend Lutherans against efforts to abolish foreign languages in the United States due to the war hysteria. Accusations of pro-Germanism against the Lutheran church were brought before the Judiciary Committee of the United States Senate. Midwestern state legislatures and local defense councils were threatening drastic action to prohibit the use of German—and of other foreign languages as well—in public worship and in the instruction of the young. The foreign language press was also to be abolished. An authoritative spokesman in Washington was needed to uphold Lutheran rights in areas beyond the scope of the Commission for Soldiers' and Sailors' Welfare.

Secondly, there was need for an emergency home mission ministry in the temporary communities at mushrooming munitions factories and shipyards. Here was a particularly delicate area for Lutheran cooperation since it directly involved establishing worship services and a spiritual ministry to Lutherans of all church bodies who moved into a new housing area. Government regulations required that all Protestant work be done through the interdenominational agency, the Federal Council of Churches. This meant that Lutherans had to band together in going through the Federal Council in their efforts to minister to all Lutheran industrial workers.

The third anticipated need was for aid in reconstruction among Europe's Lutherans after the destruction and spiritual chaos visited upon the lands of Europe in the great war. Without knowing in 1918 just how vast the needs of Europe's Lutherans would be, it was obvious that American Lutherans could offer more effective help in concert than by going separate ways.

Plans Are Laid

As a result of these major concerns the Executive Committee of the Commission invited the executives of all the general Lutheran bodies in America to meet in a conference of presidents and their representatives at Zion Lutheran Church, Harrisburg, Pennsylvania, on July 17, 1918, to consider a cooperative agency. It is not entirely clear from the sketchy evidence available today how this meeting was effected. Evidently,[3] the Commission Chairman, F. H. Knubel, sent telegrams setting the date and place as a preliminary notice. Then, at the request of the Commission, the President of the General Council, T. E. Schmauk, took the lead in sending a formal invitation that also carried the signature of three other presidents of general bodies: M. G. G. Scherer of the United Synod South, V. G. A. Tressler of the General Synod, and H. G. Stub of the Norwegian body. The invitation was accompanied by instructions for reaching Zion Church and these notations:

> It is suggested that each President may bring a further representative with him.
> The presentation of the problems will be made by Dr. F. H. Knubel, Chairman of the National Lutheran Commission.
> The Lutheran Bureau, also, through its secretary, Rev. O. H. Pannkoke, desires to make a proposition to the meeting of the Presidents.

The invitation itself follows:

> WHEREAS, certain vital problems of national scope have been pressing insistently upon the attention of the National Lutheran Commission for Soldiers' and Sailors' Welfare, which said Commission feels to be beyond its jurisdiction but also of the utmost and immediate importance to the welfare of all Lutherans in America; and
> WHEREAS, the said Commission has suggested to the Presidents of all Lutheran general bodies that a meeting be called for the consideration of these problems at a very early day;
> THEREFORE, following the precedent established in the creation of the National Lutheran War Commission when the then existing war agencies of the United Lutheran Church in America, and the Norwegian Lutheran Church of America,

called the Lutheran War Commission into existence, we, the undersigned, hereby respectfully call a meeting of the Presidents of all general bodies of Lutherans to be held in Zion Lutheran Church, Harrisburg, Pa., at 10:00 A.M. of July 17th, 1918.

Meanwhile O. H. Pannkoke was active toward the same end in behalf of the Lutheran Bureau. For him the concern focused upon the attacks being made in the name of patriotism upon the Lutheran church and the German language. On June 19 he sent a letter to general body presidents describing the Bureau's concern and the need for common action, ending with this paragraph:

> To attain such united action the Lutheran Bureau is calling a meeting of the presidents of the Lutheran Synods. A number of the presidents have already been seen personally and have agreed to come. Within the next weeks I shall take occasion to see you personally and discuss as well the urgency of the situation as the need of united and consistent action to meet it.

In the weeks preceding the Harrisburg meeting Pannkoke visited a number of the general body presidents as well as the National Lutheran Editorial Association. Obviously he was working hard to promote a cooperative agency.[4] He was also seeking to provide the sponsorship of such an agency for his Lutheran Bureau, a development which took place a few months after the NLC's founding.

Fifteen church leaders met at Harrisburg on July 17, 1918.[5] Present were H. G. Stub, C. H. L. Schuette, T. E. Schmauk, F. H. Knubel, C. M. Jacobs, H. A. Weller, L. Boe, V. G. A. Tressler, M. G. G. Scherer, D. H. Steffens, J. F. Wenchel, J. R. Mattson, L. Larsen, F. Jacobson, O. H. Pannkoke. Stub was appointed chairman. Knubel spoke of creating a committee or commission to represent Lutherans before non-Lutheran agencies. Pannkoke proposed joint action to face the difficulties created by the war situation for the Lutheran church. A committee was appointed to draw up resolutions over the lunch hour. The committee— Schmauk, Steffens, Boe—met and left the formulation of agreed-upon resolutions to Steffens, Missouri Synod pastor who represented the Synodical Conference. In the afternoon Steffens brought in three recommendations which were adopted with very slight emendation as the following three paragraphs.

> While we feel that some action must be taken with respect to the language question we deem it inexpedient that any public statement be made before this problem has been carefully considered in its relation to and bearing on other vital problems affecting our church and a careful study has been made of the means to be employed to produce desired results.
>
> We feel that further discussion of these problems will show the necessity of the creation of a national council or committee representing the entire Lutheran Church so far as possible, the duties, responsibilities, powers and functions of which would be clearly defined and limited.
>
> We therefore crave your permission to recommend that a committee be appointed to formulate plans for the creation of such a national council or committee of the Lutheran Church and given power to call a meeting for the consideration of any plan it may desire to present to cope with the present situation or problems arising with the reconstruction at the close of the war.

Other resolutions dealt with the creation of a well-rounded committee to carry out the third resolution and to meet at the Fort Pitt Hotel in Pittsburgh August 1.

Present for the August 1 meeting in Pittsburgh were the following presidents of Lutheran church bodies: H. G. Stub of the Norwegian Lutheran Church, F. Richter of the Iowa Synod, C. H. L. Schuette of the Joint Synod of Ohio, H. A. Weller of the Ministerium of Pennsylvania (representing the General Council), G. A. Brandelle of the Augustana Synod. Present also were C. G. Heckert representing President V. G. A. Tressler of the General Synod, and F. H. Knubel and L. Larsen representing the Commission. Stub was elected chairman and Larsen secretary, actions which were repeated at the constituting meeting in September. Knubel gave a resumé of discussions to that point. Weller presented a tentative outline for a "Lutheran Federal Council" and Schuette submitted the constitution prepared at Toledo in 1915. The committee proceeded on the basis of Weller's proposal to prepare a statement of five purposes which were essentially those later adopted for the organization. They also took action specifying that both clergymen and laymen be appointed to the council and that the Lutheran bodies authorize united appeals for funds when "special work of particular magnitude" is taken up by the council. The secretary was asked to request the presidents of all general Lutheran bodies "to appoint the proportionate representation from their Bodies for a meeting to organize the Lutheran Federal Council, to be held at the Auditorium Hotel in Chicago, Friday, September 6, 1918, at 10 o'clock A.M."

An hour before the appointed meeting of September 6 the Pittsburgh planning committee reported back to the Harrisburg group of synodical presidents. Those present—Stub, Schmauk, Brandelle, Schuette, Tressler, Richter, Knubel, and Larsen—received the Pittsburgh report and called in the delegates to constitute the new council.

The Council Organized

Thirty men[6] met in the Auditorium Hotel in Chicago, September 6, 1918, to organize the new council. Besides the Commission, the following church bodies were represented: the General Synod, the General Council, the Joint Synod of Ohio, the Synod of Iowa and Other States, the Augustana Synod, the Norwegian Lutheran Church, the Norwegian Lutheran Free Church, and the Danish Lutheran Church. Representatives of the United Synod South expressed by letter their great interest and their regrets that they could not be present. A letter was read from the Reverend D. H. Steffens of Baltimore, who had represented the Synodical Conference at the Harrisburg meeting, stating that it would not be possible for the Synodical Conference to participate in the proposed council.

President Schmauk read a paper with a proposed form of organization which became the basis for discussion and action in creating regulations for the Council. The preamble asserted that: "The undersigned, presidents and representatives of sundry General Bodies of the Lutheran Church in America, by such authority as they may possess by virtue of their office and appointment, and in view of exigencies presenting themselves upon the Church for solution, have associated themselves together for the purpose and upon and subject to the terms and conditions following." The name chosen was National Lutheran Council. The purposes, in keeping with those presented by Weller at Pittsburgh, were to promote, as far as possible:

1. True and uniform statistical information concerning the Lutheran Church in America.

2. Publicity in all matters that require common utterance by the Lutheran Church.

3. Representation of our Church in its relation to entities outside of itself, without prejudice to the confessional basis of any participating body, as well as bringing home to the Church a consciousness of general and specific needs for attention and action.

4. Activities dealing with, or the creation of agencies to deal with, the problems arising out of war and other emergencies where no such common Lutheran agencies now exist, and to coordinate, harmonize, and unify the activities of existing agencies.

5. The coordination of activities and agencies of the Lutheran Church in America for the solution of problems arising from social, economic, intellectual or other conditions or changes affecting religious life and consciousness.

6. The fostering of true Christian loyalty and the maintenance of a righteous relation between Church and State as separate entities with correlated yet distinctly defined functions.

Each participating body was to have one representative on the council for every one hundred thousand confirmed members or one-third fraction thereof. All actions were to be subject to the approval of the member bodies. Action was taken to place the headquarters in New York City, and provision was made for conducting general campaigns for funds for emergency purposes. It was agreed that expenses for maintaining the council would be borne by the bodies on a per capita basis.

First officers elected for the council were: president, H. G. Stub; vice president, John L. Zimmerman; secretary, Lauritz Larsen. The executive committee chose Ernest F. Eilert to be treasurer. Other members of the executive committee chosen were: Knubel, Schuette, Brandelle, and Weller. In December Richter of the Iowa Synod was added to the executive committee. Fifteen articles were adopted by the assembled group, incorporating the above agreements and providing the "Regulations" by which the new council was to be governed.

Launched Into Action

In this manner the National Lutheran Council was launched on a forty-eight year course of pioneering in American Lutheran cooperation. One could say that the Council *sprang* into existence, for its leaders moved rapidly. The Council was a going concern less than a year after creation of the wartime emergency Commission. Less than two months after the first planning session the Council was constituted. Furthermore, one could say that the Council sprang into *action*. It was born running. World events and the prior activities of the Commission gave the Council a full agenda from the start. Before the end of 1918 the Council held a home missions conference and another full Council meeting as well as two meetings of the executive committee. All these were national meetings in a day when travel was more difficult than it is now. Obviously the Council came into being because of a sense of urgency shared by many Lutherans.

What is more, the participating presidents of general Lutheran bodies were acting rather boldly, at least some of them exceeding their explicit constitutional authority. They acted, according to the preamble, "by such authority as they may possess" and "in view of exigencies." It took months, and in some cases years, before their bodies could ratify their actions. Meanwhile the Council had launched programs and a national campaign for funds.

When the responsible heads of church bodies act in such a precipitous manner, it reflects a real pioneering spirit, a worthy anticipation of the trends in churchmanship in the twentieth century. In fact, the National Lutheran Council was begun as a venture of faith.

Why could these men hope that their actions, used by the Holy Spirit, would succeed in meeting significant responsibilities

through Lutheran cooperation? These reasons have been outlined in this chapter. In church mergers and in Reformation celebrations one could detect a still-timid but growing solidarity
among America's Lutherans. Besides, the pressures of war and
postwar disruptions—only dimly sensed as the beginning of a new
age—posed urgent human problems which put into fresh perspectives the former controversies among Lutheran groups. And
the work of the wartime Commission had started to dispel some
of the suspicion which set the leaders of one group off from those
of another.

In that manner it happened that in the fall of 1918 Lutheran
leaders bound themselves together for concerted action through
a new Council. Some parts of Lutheranism remained aloof and
soon criticized. Criticism and opposition were quickly voiced
within many of the participating bodies. Some of the leaders
who took the step did so with serious questions of their own
and even possessed of grave doubts about the wisdom of this
move. Deep doubts that touch upon conscience do not disappear
because of formal actions or full agendas. They have to be *lived
through*. In the National Lutheran Council they were lived
through *in concert*.

II

Establishing Domestic Patterns

(1918-1925)

Bold action brought the National Lutheran Council into existence in rapid steps, mainly because it had an urgent agenda before it was launched. This meant that on its shakedown voyage the Council was already bearing unusually heavy freight. That it came through its earliest years in sound condition is a testimony to the wisdom of its leaders and to a will-to-cooperate on the part of many American Lutherans.

As we have noted, the three immediate issues were the ministry to temporary communities, the language question, and postwar relief for overseas churches. Each of these quickly assumed larger dimensions in keeping with the broad purposes outlined in the Council's Regulations. Meanwhile inner tensions arose, reflecting differing ideas about an agency for inter-Lutheran cooperation.

Attitudes About Cooperation

Broadly, four attitudes about cooperation are discernible among America's Lutherans in the early twentieth century. One large group felt that any cooperation without complete agreement in doctrine and in practice compromised one's witness to the truth and must be rejected. It was this viewpoint which caused Missouri Synod and Synodical Conference Lutherans to turn down the invitation to form a council. They had not joined the wartime Commission, though they did agree to limited coordination of their own work with that of the Commission because of dire emergency, sheer courtesy, and the necessities of relating to the government.

A second group—best represented by the Iowa Synod in this story—believed that, lacking complete theological agreement, limited cooperation with other Lutherans was possible in certain areas of activity—such as emergency deeds of mercy and relations with the government—without compromise of one's witness to the truth. These areas of activity were termed external matters (*res externae*). Other areas of activity, internal matters (*res internae*), such as worshiping together or sharing Lutheran pastors across denominational lines, would be compromising one's witness to the truth and hence would be unacceptable cooperative activities. Only after complete theological agreement and a formal statement of pulpit and altar fellowship between two general synods could they cooperate in such internal matters. People of this viewpoint were insistent that the National Lutheran Council should stick strictly to external matters. Unfortunately, this distinction was hard to make with any precision or agreement and almost impossible to apply in the face of emergency appeals for help.

A third and similar viewpoint—represented by H. G. Stub in early National Lutheran Council days—also stressed the external-internal distinction but wanted the National Lutheran Council to seek doctrinal consensus in order to be able to move into cooperation in more internal areas of church life.

A fourth group, found most strongly within the United Lutheran Church but not limited to that body, felt that Lutherans in America already shared enough doctrinal agreement, in common subscription to the historic confessions, to cooperate freely where needed.

At the organizational meeting in September 1918, Article II, setting forth the six purposes, was adopted with the understanding that the executive committee could improve the phraseology. The first executive committee meeting therefore focused on "scope and plans" for the National Lutheran Council. President Stub led off by voicing his hesitancies and mentioning the problems in defining the National Lutheran Council's role. Some bodies, including his own, he maintained, would need to be shown the necessity for the Council in contrast to the wartime Commission which served an obvious need. The National Lutheran Council, as an "after war emergency organization," would go far beyond the immediate problems and thus needed to be clearly defined. It was not a federation based on repeated doctrinal discussions and could not speak for a united Lutheran church on doctrinal matters "but only an organization dealing with matters of a more external character." Stub concluded that "it is my earnest hope that the Council may be a great help in bringing the different Lutheran church bodies together in a great American Lutheran Church; but we must go slowly."

President Stub was torn two ways, between his sincere desire to cooperate in tackling urgent tasks and his conviction that careful doctrinal discussion and agreement must precede cooperation in "internal matters." In this ambivalence he not only represented the conservative majority in his own Norwegian Lutheran Church in America but also the vast majority among the midwestern Lutherans who were not in the Synodical Conference. It is of great significance for the National Lutheran Council's life, and for the course of twentieth century American Lutheranism, that Stub, despite his doubts, served faithfully as President for two years and continued to be actively interested thereafter. In working together Lutherans came to trust fellow Lutherans across synodical boundaries.

Two Approaches to Cooperation

These inner tensions were exposed in the first actions demanded of the new Council as it took up the ministry to temporary communities. This was work already initiated by the wartime Commission. But questions were raised when a permanent Council assumed these tasks at the war's end. For it was clear that home missions work, providing worship services and pastoral care for many migrant Lutherans, involved recognition of one synod's ministry by the other general bodies. Yet circumstances were forcing a united Lutheran approach.

To face this issue the executive committee brought together representatives of the home mission boards of National Lutheran Council bodies in December in Columbus, Ohio. Here it was agreed that the National Lutheran Council continue this work but that effort be made to turn over particular projects to the several home missions boards as rapidly as possible. All that need be said about this whole program is that it was harmoniously carried through by the National Lutheran Council until the need for such services disappeared in the early 1920's.

But at the same December meeting two other suggestions were made by the home missions executives to the National Lutheran Council. They represent two contrasting approaches to cooperation. Both were tried. One was a request to the presidents of co-operating bodies to appoint "a joint committee to confer on questions of doctrine and practice, with a view to the coordination of their home mission and other work." This procedure was adopted at H. G. Stub's urging. The second request was that "in the interim, the Mission Boards of the various Lutheran Bodies be asked, and are expected, as a matter of courtesy to the other bodies, to confer with the boards of those Synods or general bodies represented in or near the locality where the mission work is to be begun, before the work is started." This latter was the idea which led to the Lutheran Home Missions Council of America (organized in 1931) and the comity agreements among National Lutheran Council bodies whereby coordinated planning could replace open competition in the planting of new congregations in America.

Since the doctrinal discussions of the first suggestion did not produce agreement, the whole of National Lutheran Council history was "in the interim" of such comity agreements. Furthermore, the suggestion of gathering home missions executives in a loose conference to coordinate their planning was picked up by foreign missions executives the following year (Lutheran Foreign Missions Conference) and by welfare executives and other groupings at later dates. These cooperative conferences, using National Lutheran Council staff and other services, have been both powerful and fruitful in providing coordinated and cooperative approaches to their tasks in forwarding the variegated mission of the church. Such informal organizations, bringing together the responsible decision-makers in any particular area of Lutheran activity, have not only been a major factor in the movement of Lutheran cooperation. They have also been a potent force working for harmony and unity of spirit among America's Lutherans.

Doctrinal Conferences

At the suggestion of the home missions conference of December 1918, and the mandate of the second annual meeting of the National Lutheran Council the following day, two important conferences of doctrinal discussion were held. For these conferences a second agenda item had been indicated by the annual meeting, namely, "to prepare a statement which shall define the essentials of a catholic spirit as viewed by the Lutheran Church." Knubel had asked for this action in view of the question of relations with the Federal Council of Churches, the YMCA, and other religious bodies in the great problems of postwar reconstruction.

The Joint Committee on Doctrine and Practice held its first meeting March 11-13, 1919, at Chicago. Eighteen committee members were present, representing seven general bodies. First Knubel read a paper on "the Essentials of a True Catholic Spirit." Then papers were read by H. E. Jacobs, C. H. L. Schuette, and H. G. Stub, discussing the issues from the standpoint of their respective church bodies. Schuette's paper dealt with the principles of comity agreements in home missions. Since Stub's paper dealt with more basic doctrinal matters, it was discussed first.

The whole meeting was taken up with the point-by-point discussion, amendment, and adoption of Stub's paper.[1] The resulting document, which became known as the Chicago Theses, was reported to the National Lutheran Council with the recommendation that it be referred to the general bodies with commendation. The Committee also referred Schuette's paper to the Council, requested that the papers by Knubel and Jacobs be published,[2] and referred Knubel's paper to a committee of three— Knubel, Stub, and T. E. Schmauk—to prepare statements on the subject for a future meeting of the Joint Committee.

Stub was hoping that his statement would lead to doctrinal

consensus upon which the National Lutheran Council could go beyond "externals" and take up cooperative missions activity. In his introductory remarks he asked:

> Would it not be possible to get a mutual declaration regarding doctrine and practice that would be satisfactory to the representatives of the Council? And if this should prove possible, could not this declaration be laid before the different church bodies, recommending, on the basis of the mutual declaration, to these bodies to sanction the organization and the work of the Council, and even state their opinion regarding a possible coordination of home mission work wherever required by local conditions, and to some extent a certain cooperation in foreign mission work, where it would be absolutely needed?

The National Lutheran Council President was too sanguine. At the meeting R. C. H. Lenski (Joint Synod of Ohio) opposed this approach, urging that the first consideration should be "what are the matters of cooperation in externis that properly belong to the Council." He felt the Council should be simply a clearinghouse distributing the work to the various synods. Besides, in a few months the Iowa Synod withdrew from the Council because the Council failed to limit its activities to externals and Stub's own Norwegian body registered considerable opposition to the Council's role even in its more minimal and external mandate. On the other hand, ULCA people were not interested in adopting doctrinal theses as a basis for Council work, since they felt Lutherans already had all the agreement needed for cooperation. What they wanted was agreement on the principles to govern relationships with non-Lutheran religious bodies.

Underlying these disagreements were deeper differences of outlook. This became evident the following January (1920) when the Joint Committee on Doctrine and Practice met in Chicago for a second session. Whereas Stub's theses in 1919 had dealt briefly with several basic theological teachings that had been cause for controversy in midwestern Lutheran history, this gathering dealt with "the essentials of a catholic spirit" as set forth more lengthily by Knubel and Charles M. Jacobs (substituting for an ailing Schmauk). In contrast to the Chicago Theses which were adopted, the 1920 meeting produced no agreement. Though Stub had been on the preliminary committee to prepare the report, he did not sign it and led an attack upon it. Though the discussions were amicable, they revealed deep-running differences which have remained troublesome throughout National Lutheran Council history.

The Knubel-Jacobs document consisted of five parts. In the first part the authors set forth their understanding of the catholicity of the church, as drawn from the Lutheran confessions, and the reasons why one group of Christians must define its relationship to other groups which bear the name of the church. This section concludes by asserting that a particular group of Christians must approach other groups sincerely seeking agreements in understanding of the Gospel and willing to cooperate in works of serving love so long as it is free to give its testimony to what it holds to be the truth. Part two stated that, since all Lutheran bodies represented at the conference subscribe to the Lutheran confessions, they are all in the unity of the faith and together form one church. The third part rejected any Lutheran participation in the movements toward organic union among Protestants.

Part four asserted willingness to cooperate with other Protestant bodies in activities that belong to the church's work so long as there is no denial of conviction or suppression of testimony to the truth. As "a positive basis of practical cooperation" eight broad doctrinal principles were set down. The fifth part condemned certain "false teachings," asking Lutheran people to reject those groups with teachings contradictory to the eight doctrines already set forth.

In explaining his objections to this report Stub repeated his hope that a brief doctrinal statement like the Chicago Theses would provide enough consensus to allow the National Lutheran Council to proceed with tasks that went beyond external matters. His concern to receive the approval of Missouri Synod Lutherans was revealed in his reference [3] to the favorable judgment put upon the Chicago Theses by *Lehre und Wehre*, journal of that synod.

His first objection to the present report on essentials of a catholic spirit was that it was too long and would be difficult for church

bodies to adopt. He also objected (1) to reference to works of
serving love as marks of the church, (2) to the statement that no
single group of Christians has ever possessed all the attributes
of the one, holy, catholic and apostolic church, (3) to the asser-
tion that subscription to the Lutheran confessions unites bodies
without further doctrinal discussion, and, (4) chiefly, to the listing of eight doctrinal principles as a basis for cooperation beyond
Lutheranism without stressing the Trinity, the Scriptures as inspired and inerrant, and, above all, the characteristic Lutheran
doctrine of the Lord's Supper. In other words, Stub was opposed
to any cooperation with other religious groups that did not involve agreement on the doctrines peculiar to Lutheranism. Without doubt he spoke for the large proportion of midwestern Lutheranism in espousing this viewpoint.

The Knubel-Jacobs paper was discussed and amended but
never adopted by the Joint Committee. In an altered form it was
adopted later that year by the ULCA as its "Washington Declaration" by which that body has been guided in its external relations.
Within three months after the second meeting (January 1920)
of the Joint Committee, there was agreement among the presidents of National Lutheran Council participating bodies to have
no more meetings of the committee, to refrain from using the
phrase *res externae,* and to discard the Chicago Theses for the
time being.[4] The way of doctrinal discussion as an approach to
cooperation soon reached a dead end. It revealed a split within
the youthful Council that could easily have destroyed that agency
and dispersed the movement for Lutheran cooperation. The se-
verest test was to come a decade later. In 1920 differences were
dropped in the interest of getting necessary tasks done. One body,
the Iowa Synod, withdrew.

The differences were long-standing socio-historical ones. Midwestern Lutherans were quite suspicious of eastern Lutherans,
since the latter had a longer history in this country and were more
Americanized, more friendly toward the non-Lutherans around
them. Besides, it was not forgotten that a century earlier eastern
Lutheranism had been almost devoid of loyalty to the Lutheran
confessions.

The differences were also ideological, i.e., the use of ideas and phrases to serve group purposes. On the American scene in general the term "hyphenated-American" was a belittling one. In the sharp Modernist-Fundamentalist controversy of the day those who did not speak of Scripture as "inerrant" were accused of destroying the Word of God. In Lutheran circles the epithet "Unionism" (yoking oneself carelessly with those of a different confession) was hurled at the ULCA because that body favored Lutheran merger without further doctrinal discussion and was willing to enter into limited church cooperation with non-Lutherans. Even the term "United" in the ULCA name reminded some midwesterners of the union churches of Germany with their linking of Lutherans with those of the Reformed persuasion.

Speaking of the Norwegian Lutheran Church of America in 1920, its historian states that "together with other Midwest Lutherans it was *practically* related to the ULCA, but *sociologically* and *ideologically* related to the Missouri Synod." [5]

Both sociological and ideological differences lost their divisive power when loyal Lutherans worked with one another across synodical lines in the National Lutheran Council. Without this trust-inspiring process doctrinal discussions became controversies instead of pathways to unity. This truth is one of the great legacies which the National Lutheran Council hands on after nearly five decades of experience. By 1920 the process was only begun; fortunately, it continued despite strains.

Theological Differences

There were serious theological differences as well among Lutherans in the National Lutheran Council. These distinguished one general body from another, but they were also finding expression as internal differences within most of the bodies. The gaps were not nearly so great as they had been in the nineteenth century, since virtually all Lutherans subscribed to the Lutheran confessions. But by 1920 there were two major ways of interpreting Lutheran theology, two schools of thought. The first was "Repristination Theology." [6] This position, given decisive formulation in nineteenth century Germany, sought to recover the pure treasures of Lutheran thought by returning to the dogmaticians of seventeenth century scholastic orthodoxy. Originally a romantic reaction against rationalism, in twentieth century America it became the rigid defense of a static, detailed system of scholastic orthodoxy in which, however, certain controverted points became decisive in identifying fellow Lutherans. The main hinge-points were the verbal inspiration of Scripture and the use of the confessions as documents legally binding on Lutheran consciences. By the 1920's this position was easily confused with Fundamentalism in many Lutheran minds. Like the Fundamentalists, Repristination theologians rejected the findings of the scholarship known as biblical criticism and refused any cooperation with those who did not accept their hinge-points of doctrine, their particular list of fundamentals. At the turn of the century Repristination Theology was virtually unchallenged among American Lutherans.

Meanwhile, in nineteenth century German theology, romanticism in reaction to rationalism had also produced an "Erlangen School." This school, stressing personal Christian experience, took a more dynamic approach to Lutheran theology and was more likely to emphasize sixteenth century roots rather than the seventeenth century systematicians. Instead of seeing Scripture as verbally inspired, Erlangen theologians thought of it as revealing God's redemptive activity in history (Heilsgeschichte). They were therefore more open to the new biblical criticism. And they considered the Lutheran confessions as historically conditioned rather than as legalistically binding documents. Instead of viewing Lutheran theology as a closed system these men were inclined to view it organically, with a central truth around which other doctrines take their place, some of them being more peripheral. By the time of the formation of the ULCA in 1918 aspects of the Erlangen theology were influential among its leaders. Especially Charles M. Jacobs took the lead in giving Erlangen's hermeneutical viewpoint to the basic ULCA documents. It was the Erlangen influence which enabled Knubel and Jacobs to stress the catholicity of the Lutheran confessions and to present a position that favored limited cooperation with non-Lutheran church bodies.

When leaders of the National Lutheran Council talked theology in earnest, an exclusivist Repristination Theology confronted a more catholic, Erlangen-influenced theology that interpreted Scripture and confessions historically. No compromise was possible. It was the part of wisdom to break off discussion. Continued cooperation in deeds of mercy and in a combined approach to the public reflected a growing sense of fellowship that continued to bridge the evident gap. It was fellowship in a common urgent mission.

Representing Lutheranism

Meanwhile, the basic fabric of National Lutheran Council existence was established during its first seven years in its domestic, homeland programs. Home mission work in temporary communities, as we have seen, both provoked theological discussion and led into a Lutheran Home Missions Conference through which home missions executives of various bodies have for decades coordinated their programs to avoid competition and overlapping in establishing new congregations. Actual services in temporary communities were either disbanded or turned over to an appropriate synod within a few years.

The second pressing homefront issue in 1918 was the language question, the threat of legislation prohibiting use of the German language. At its December meeting the National Lutheran Council adopted a lengthy, carefully-worded statement that supported "sane plans for the Americanization of immigrant and foreign elements" but called attention to "the injustice and transgression which result from an inconsiderate attempt to infringe upon the liberty of the Christian to have the Gospel ministered unto him in a language which his heart and mind can best comprehend."

However, the real thrust of the National Lutheran Council in representing Lutherans before the government lay in establishing enduring contacts in Washington. The Secretary of the National Lutheran Council, Lauritz Larsen, was put in charge of a Washington office. His duties were to keep in constant touch with various governmental officials and agencies in order to help protect the rights of Lutherans and in order to interpret Lutheran viewpoints in the postwar world. Early in 1919 Larsen became

General Secretary and continued as chief executive officer until his death in 1923. From the start National Lutheran Council headquarters were in New York City where it used the facilities of the wartime Commission. By mid-1919 Larsen's office was in New York where he also carried responsibilities for the Commission for three years. At the same time he continued active representation in Washington.

Attacks on the German language quickly faded after the war, but a Lutheran voice in Washington has continued to prove valuable in a number of ways. For example, passports for a variety of overseas assignments were more readily secured when the responsible officials knew a Lutheran leader and learned from him the reasons why prompt or unusual clearance was needed. During the early 1920's Lutherans by National Lutheran Council action threw their support behind a bill in Congress to secure uniform laws on marriage and divorce in the United States by way of an amendment to the Constitution. In Larsen's letter to congressmen urging passage of this particular bill he affirmed separation of church and state but included marriage and divorce laws as one of "certain fundamental moral questions over which the State has control, in the settlement of which the conviction of the Church should be considered." [7] Another action in which direct pressure was brought to bear upon public officials was an effort in 1922 to keep the government from a too drastic reduction of the number of chaplains for the army.

Washington contacts also were helpful when the NLC had reason to go before foreign governments. On one occasion, for example, Council officials were readily able to contact the proper French officials to secure permission to conduct relief work in the occupied territory of the Ruhr. Another time diplomatic representatives of the Latvian government were approached to plead the Lutheran cause in the unsuccessful effort to keep St. James Church in Riga from being taken over by the Roman Catholics.[8] These are but two of numerous examples.

A different kind of representation in behalf of Lutherans was carried through in these same years to protect the public image of Lutherans by changing a textbook statement. In their *History of the United States* Charles and Mary Beard, discussing wartime United States, had stated: "The German language press . . . the National German Alliance, minor German societies, and Lutheran churches came to the support of the German cause." At the behest of the executive committee of the Council Larsen protested, so that Beard apologized,[9] and the word Lutheran was changed to German in the next printing with the promise that thereafter the word "some" would be inserted before "German churches." An NLC committee was appointed to keep a watch on history textbooks for misrepresentations.

Larsen and succeeding executives also spent much time and energy representing Lutheranism in inter-religious programs. A great variety of *ad hoc* committees, seeking to carry through specific religious activities on a broad interdenominational or civic basis, wanted a Lutheran at their meetings or at least on their letterhead. Larsen and his successors tried conscientiously to keep in touch with such groups when they were working in areas of Lutheran involvement. Especially in coordinating committees for overseas relief—where exchange of information was particularly needed—National Lutheran Council men played a leading role. However, they tried to keep out of the limelight because religious cooperation with non-Lutherans was a sensitive, potentially divisive subject in the NLC constituency. Sometimes they were put on a committee without prior opportunity to decline. This they strenuously resisted. In their correspondence they frequently remonstrated, for example, with Charles S. Macfarland, General Secretary of the Federal Council of Churches, because he made them appear more committed to the Federal Council and to specific parts of its work than they actually were. Yet it is clear that these men felt an urgent responsibility, within the announced purposes of NLC, to represent Lutherans in many worthy inter-religious undertakings. Over the years the NLC had extended contacts with such organizations as the Interchurch World Movement, the Laymen's Missionary Movement, the World Alliance for International Friendship through the Churches, the World Conference on Faith and Order, and above all, the Federal Council of the Churches of Christ in America.

This kind of Lutheran voice in governmental, public, and inter-religious affairs has characterized the role of the National Lutheran Council throughout its half century of history.

Publicity Work

Publicity work is another form of public relations which has been basic to the NLC program from start to finish. Back in 1914 some Missouri Lutherans in New York City formed the American Lutheran Publicity Bureau which has for more than five decades had wide influence, especially in the national dissemination of tracts for use by congregations. In 1915, as we have seen, an inter-Lutheran society in the same city organized a Reformation Quadricentenary Committee from which there emerged in 1917 the Lutheran Bureau. Under the direction of Otto H. Pannkoke the Bureau was the pioneer religious news agency in the United States. With the formation of the National Lutheran Council the Bureau offered its services and by the spring of 1919 it had become the publicity arm of the NLC, continuing under the direction of Pannkoke until the end of the following year. Other early executives in this work were the Reverend Howard R. Gold, the Reverend Frank E. Jensen and Winfred P. Elson.

The central feature of the bureau's work was the gathering and dissemination of news about Lutherans and the Lutheran church. News items were released at frequent intervals to metropolitan dailies across the country. Other news stories were sent to the church press. News copy was mailed to a network of Lutheran pastors who were to add local items and take it personally to the editor of the local newspaper. Effort was made to encourage Lutherans to become publicity conscious in order to project a positive image of Lutheranism before the public. The bureau maintained a vast file of clippings as evidence of the effectiveness of its services. One of the major facets of the bureau's work has been providing publicity for special Lutheran events. Many conventions of church bodies, for example, have been given expert publicity management by the NLC staff. The best methods used by secular news agencies have been put to use by the news bureau, providing an outstanding NLC service to Lutheranism over all its years.

Statistics and Information

A third form of public relations carried on by the Council was in the area of research, statistics, and information. Less spectacular than the representative voice before the public or the publicity and news services, this branch of work, nonetheless, has had a considerable impact over the years, both in shaping a positive public image of Lutheranism and in helping Lutherans to a more confident, accurate, and united self-image.

In its early years this work was the responsibility of the Reverend George L. Kieffer and the Reverend O. M. Norlie. Kieffer became one of the leaders in the field of religious statistics in the United States. Gathering all kinds of information about Lutherans, building up a reference library, providing accurate information in response to questions from staff people, pastors, or outsiders were routine tasks faithfully carried out to the enrichment of American Lutheranism by the increase of helpful knowledge. Accurate and standardized statistical information about Lutherans was not available prior to 1918. Over the years great progress has been made in providing uniform categories and in teaching Lutherans the importance of an accurate reporting of statistics. An organization for Lutheran statisticians formed in 1917 received strong Council support for its conferences and other activities. The NLC made formal requests to the United States Census Bureau for changes in its 1930 census procedures in order to reflect Lutheran strength more accurately.

But the most concrete and influential contribution of Kieffer and Norlie was the series of eight editions, between 1921 and 1937, of the *Lutheran World Almanac*. Running to nearly one thousand pages in 1921, though subsequent editions were smaller, these volumes were widely circulated. They were quite useful in libraries, at newsdesks of newspapers and magazines, in pastors' studies, wherever reference materials were needed. Combining the features of an almanac, an encyclopedia, and an annual, they provided a vast storehouse of all kinds of information about Lutherans: their history, their geography, their organizations, their leaders. American Lutheranism received more detailed coverage from the start but world Lutheranism was given increasingly

accurate descriptions. This was an ambitious undertaking for a
new organization with a precarious budget. Eventually, after
1937, it was discontinued because of the costs.

Both the dissemination of news and the work with statistics
and the *Almanac* were pioneer activities about which it can accurately be said that they made Lutheran history.

Fund Appeals

Early appeals for funds by the National Lutheran Council were
also ground-breaking achievements. Here again Pannkoke and
Kieffer were key workers, together with Walton H. Greever, who
later became secretary of the ULCA. The first fund-raising effort
was carried through by the wartime Commission in the winter
of 1918. It had the tremendous heart-appeal of following the boys
in military service into camps and overseas. But it also took concerted planning that crossed synodical lines and mobilized many
workers over a continent. The collection of $1,350,000—nearly
doubling the goal—was a momentous boost to Lutheran self-
esteem and to the budding movement of cooperative Lutheranism.

One year later, when the National Lutheran Council needed
large sums of money for overseas relief and for the emergency
support of former German missions, the same men and methods,
including a network of state chairmen, were utilized. More than
$600,000 was raised in that winter of 1919. In the fall was
launched a successful campaign for 2,000 tons of usable clothing.
Beginning in 1920 the reoccurring campaigns for funds and
clothing were called World Service Appeals. In 1920 the goal
was $1,800,000. Methods became still more intensive by working
through the auxiliary organizations of the churches to reach
every segment of Lutheran church life with the story of need
and the call for help.

However, repeated appeals met with greater lethargy and resistance in an increasingly blasé postwar America. Some of the
appeals fell far short of their goal. One grass-roots summary in
1923 gave three reasons why people were not so generous:
(1) they are doubting whether conditions in Europe continue

to be as bad as they are painted; (2) they say they have given repeatedly—let Europeans care for themselves; and (3) they say Europeans have outraged God and cannot really be helped until they turn to him once more.[10] Before 1925 it was clear that the phase of generous help from America, including America's Lutherans, for a ravaged Europe had passed.

Nonetheless, these great appeals were a major and unprecedented achievement for American Lutherans working together as never before. Between 1919 and 1925 cash and clothing totaling nearly six and three-quarter millions of dollars were contributed through the National Lutheran Council. It was a vast outpouring from the hearts and hands of millions of Lutherans. It showed the strength of united action. It also helped to turn American Lutheranism into a more self-confident, outgoing, giving body of Christians. Their sights were raised.

Lauritz Larsen

Lauritz Larsen stood at the center of all National Lutheran Council activities from their beginning until his tragic death at the age of forty in January 1923. As the youthful representative in Washington of the wartime Commission he had inspired such confidence that he was given the same role when the Council came into existence. In a few months he was also given the chief executive post of the National Lutheran Council. In December of 1920 he was elected president while continuing his executive duties.

Larsen's voluminous correspondence and the many testimonials at his death attest to the great esteem he enjoyed among churchmen and public officials in America and abroad.[11] Herbert Hoover, with whom he had close association, referred to him as "one of the finest type of an American citizen." Nathan Söderblom, famous Archbishop of the Church of Sweden, stated that Larsen "possessed qualities that made him a leader and a source of strength in the Household of Christ."

The Council's chief executive was hard-working, wise, and humane. One who reads his correspondence marvels at his patience in handling details, his concern for the requests of individuals, combined with a persistent idealism and ability to keep the broadest aims in view.

In one instance a series of letters flowed between Larsen and an American who wanted $50 delivered to his aged parents in a remote area of Romania. After several unsuccessful efforts at delivering the money, Larsen himself took time during a European trip to deliver the money in the form of food packages to the grateful parents.[12] On the other hand, he looked steadily beyond money and acts of relief to the broader spiritual implications of Council work. He kept insisting that the Council was not so much conducting financial campaigns as it was transmitting appeals for help, that its Commissioners in Europe were not so much agents of relief as they were ambassadors from American Lutheranism to beleaguered European brethren. Always he saw the Council as a unifying force within American Lutheranism.

Lauritz Larsen was above all the home office statesman of early Council days. He took pains to give careful answers to all criticisms. And there were many critics of the National Lutheran Council as a new and often bold organization. Some of them were small but annoying—as when the NLC was sued for mishandling a package that failed to reach its European destination. Others were more serious misunderstandings or distortions—as the repeated and false accusation that an unreasonably high percentage of appeal funds went into administration.

Having been a pastor in Brooklyn, New York, Larsen knew how to work in close concert with eastern and ULCA churchmen. At the same time, as a respected member of the Norwegian Lutheran Church in America, he was able to relate to midwestern ways of thinking and to counter the repeated accusation that the Council was dominated by the ULCA. At one point, for example, he discussed with President Stub whether Council headquarters should not be in Washington rather than New York since the latter was ULCA headquarters. It is evident that Larsen went to great pains to hold Stub's loyalty to the budding Council. He played a statesman's role in maintaining peace within the Council and in keeping its programs moving in the right direction despite all emergencies. Had a lesser man held Larsen's post the Council could have foundered.

Larsen gave unstinting energy and enthusiasm to the overseas work of the National Lutheran Council. A five-month whirlwind European trip probably weakened his resistance to the sickness that caused his death. And he died while on a circuit of speeches for the World Service Appeal. But his main contribution lay in guiding the Council into successful patterns of domestic operation.

The Steady Rhythm

In summary, a movement toward a more cooperative Lutheranism in America gave birth to the National Lutheran Council as its agency. Doubts, distrust, and disagreement limited the areas of its effectiveness in the early years. Yet in the broad reaches of public relations the NLC served Lutherans and served the nation in behalf of Lutherans in a way that greatly enhanced the image of Lutheranism in America and helped Lutherans to take their full place on the American scene. And the Council did establish common bonds of association among most Lutherans on this continent.

True, from the start the Council had more spectacular success as an organization to administer overseas relief. But its leaders were always anxious to point out that their purposes went beyond emergency relief. Thus, for example, in 1922 they carefully divided the purposes and budget of the Council to show that there were two kinds of programs, "Regular Work" and "Emergency Work." And even in their momentous tasks of mercy performed overseas they were, intentionally or not, helping to forge a common consciousness among America's Lutherans. This was the steady rhythm, the substantial underpinning of National Lutheran Council accomplishments.

III

A Dramatic Overseas Role (1918-1925)

Even before its birth the National Lutheran Council had as its most pressing agenda item the impending demand for concerted action to meet emergency needs for relief and reconstruction in Europe at the war's end. While the Council was being constituted, its predecessor, the Soldiers' and Sailors' Commission, finally received clearance to send two representatives to France. They were the Reverend Charles J. Smith and the Honorable Frank M. Riter. Later the Reverend M. J. Stolee joined them in this work. These men quickly got in touch with leaders of the French Lutheran church and, finding that group in dire straits, provided immediate financial help that was termed the "practical salvation" of French Lutheranism. Such help was obviously only the beginning, however. Thus in its overseas role—as in all its early tasks—the Council found itself thoroughly involved in its very first months.

Nor were the tasks simple. It was not just a matter of channeling money and supplies overseas to meet raw human needs. That call was a compelling one for the whole American public, and Lutherans were quick to respond on that level. But in this emergency American Lutherans were becoming aware of their distinctive responsibility toward the lands and peoples from which they had sprung, since they or their fathers had emigrated from these European countries a few decades or centuries earlier. There were ties of kinship and ethnic indebtedness.

Confessional Concern

Leaders of the Council were even more conscious of confessional ties. Many of these Europeans in desperate circumstances were loyal Lutherans, even strongly confessional Lutherans with a kindred spirit. Or they were lax Lutherans who could be encouraged to strengthen their confessional loyalties as they rebuilt their shattered church life. A desire to strengthen the hands of Lutheran Christians and thereby serve the Gospel was a strong motive in this work.

In addition, it should be noted, Lutherans in America were possessed of a bit of the crusading spirit which had run so strongly in their compatriots in fighting the war. Out of deep faith and out of the convictions and scars formed by a century of theological controversy, the leaders of American Lutheranism after the war were ready to undertake reconstruction in Europe that would look toward a stronger confessional Lutheranism as a worldwide force. The younger brother had come of age sufficiently to be willing to try his hand at guiding family affairs for the first time.

As chairman of the wartime Commission, Frederick Knubel took the lead in transferring responsibilities to the new Council. At the December 1918 meeting of the Council he introduced a resolution, asking that six men be sent to Europe to be the Council's representatives. The secretary summarized his remarks as follows:

> He spoke of the great possibilities opening before our church and called attention to the fact that the Lutheran Church in America was today the strongest Lutheran Church in the world, the most orthodox, and the only part of the Lutheran Church that had learned to live under a democratic government. These facts make our duty to exert as much of international influence as possible the greater.

Knubel added that, while the need for material help for the Lutheran church is great, "the greatest help is that which we can give because of our firm Lutheran position." He then reminded his listeners that other denominations were raising funds for overseas work "largely in Lutheran lands" and pointed to "the struggle now going on in France between the conservative confessional Lutheranism and radical rationalism."

These sentiments, and the action intended, met a hearty response. Much more difficult, however, was the process of establishing a strategy. Should this European Commission simply investigate and report, or should it be empowered to grant financial aid? Should it go to non-belligerent nations—Sweden, for example? Should it limit its offer of succor to Lutheran groups of the strictest confessional rectitude, or should it offer aid to territorial churches and to theological schools that are only loosely Lutheran in order that they be not lost entirely before the onslaughts of rationalism, secularism, and Bolshevism?

Instructions for the European Commissioners, as finally adopted by the executive committee the following March, were rather broad: they were to learn and report concerning the present ecclesiastical situation of each Lutheran group in European lands involved in the war; they were to convey greetings from the Lutheran Church in America and assurances of "ready willingness to participate in the solution of their ecclesiastical problems"; and they were empowered to spend up to $50,000 before receiving further approval from the executive committee.

President Richter of the Iowa Synod added some further and private instructions which were included in the minutes "as an expression of the consensus of opinion of the committee." Underlining that NLC help should go to "those Lutheran brethren that adhere to the old faith," he took the example of the *"Protestgemeinden"* that had arisen in opposition to the liberalism of the official church in Alsace, asserting that "it would be the duty of the NLC to assist those faithful Lutherans that would organize a free church of their own in Alsace." Similarly, in Germany help should go to those of the "old faith" whose faithful Lutheranism will cause them to form a free church, cutting loose from the liberal pastors. In actual practice the European Commission was unable or unwilling to satisfy the Iowa Synod's concerns at this point as well as in other regards.

The Earlier Years

Five clergymen were sent to Europe as Commissioners by the NLC in 1919. Three reached France in June: John A. Morehead (ULCA), G. A. Fandrey (Iowa Synod), and S. G. Youngert (Augustana Synod), to be followed later by George Taylor Rygh (Norwegian Church), and H. J. Schuh (Ohio Synod). From there they spread out, touching eighteen countries in all.

French Lutheranism was neither sizeable nor strong. The accession of Alsace to France after the war added a larger and quite liberal group of Lutherans, so that Americans were concerned that confessional standards be not lost. By July of 1919 $30,000 was invested in support of a deaconess home and hospital, to provide several huts for places of worship, in meeting debt obligations on Trinité Church in Paris, and the like. Larger plans were afoot to develop a system of church education, to provide theological professorships and to secure translations of Lutheran tracts and books. In the fall a delegation of French churchmen appeared by invitation in the United States and before the Council in annual meeting. Grants were made for various church institutions in France over the next several years.

Meanwhile the Lutherans of Poland became central objects of concern in the NLC relief operations. Morehead was one of the first Americans in Poland after the war, invited by Premier Ignace Jan Paderewski and travelling in the Premier's private railroad car. There he found the physical destruction and chaos so overwhelming that he asked for funds for immediate physical relief. His description of Polish needs also helped to get the clothing appeal underway. It proved impossible to stick to ecclesiastical help alone when food, clothing, and shelter were so desperately needed. As a general principle, however, even physical relief efforts of the Council were aimed at keeping pastors able to function at their posts and relieving the starkest needs in orphanages, hospitals, and other inner mission institutions.

In the fall of 1919 Bibles were prepared and shipped to Poland. An effort was made to secure American pastors who could serve Polish congregations. Steps were taken to provide Lutheran theological and devotional literature in the Polish language. Some monies were put at the disposal of the leading Lutheran official in Poland, Superintendent Julius Bursche in Warsaw, to secure certain properties from threatened seizure.

The European Commissioners had also visited Germany, Finland, and the Baltic countries and were requesting grants for emergency relief, mainly for institutions of mercy, in these lands. They returned to the United States in December of 1919 to report to the annual meeting. It was recommended that five million dollars be raised for the overseas program for the next five years. Their report stated that "in varying degrees in every land" they had found: "undernourished and homeless children, . . . millions of refugees without homes and means of living, nation-wide hunger, institutions of mercy under the burden of debt and without sufficient means to carry on their work, pastors and teachers impoverished to the point of being driven into secular work, churches and schools destroyed by shot and shell and fire. . . . "

Morehead was named chairman of the Council's European Commission and was returned to the European tasks. M. J. Stolee was also asked to return, this time representing the Council instead of the wartime Soldiers' and Sailors' Commission. In later years the Reverend A. C. Ernst, Mr. G. F. Beschorner, the Reverend W. L. Scheding, the Reverend O. C. Mees, and the Reverend O. T. Benze also served periods as Commissioners.

In May of 1921 Morehead summarized the work of relief and reconstruction in three stages.[1] For France, Czechoslovakia, Romania, Finland, and parts of Germany the heaviest tasks of the Council have been accomplished, he stated. In Poland, Austria, the Baltic states, and the large cities of Germany the NLC is now in the midst of its greatest responsibilities. He added that the "situation has not yet been saved for the Lutheran Church in these nations." The third stage, in Russia when that nation is opened to such aid, will involve perhaps the gravest tasks of the relief of untold suffering and of church reconstruction. Emphasizing in his report the dire economic and social disruptions in the Baltic states, Morehead also described efforts to keep the large and famous St. James Church (*Jacobi Kirche*) of Riga from falling into Roman Catholic hands. At that time the treasurer's report of cumulative contributions to various European countries listed as the largest amounts: $298,000 to Poland, $240,000 to Germany, and $111,000 to France.

Russia and Germany

By December of 1921 Morehead and other NLC representatives had moved into Russia as a part of the American Relief Administration, Herbert Hoover's famous organization for channeling American material aid to the needy millions of postwar Europe. Here was one of the most dramatic episodes of the NLC's overseas program. Traveling and administering food and clothing under the most primitive conditions, the Commissioners exhausted themselves and their resources contending with mass starvation, especially among the German settlements of the Volga Valley. Other pockets of Lutherans were located in the Ukraine and in southern Russia. In aggregate these were about 125 parishes composed of nearly 650 villages, perhaps a million Lutherans. For a period the Council appropriated $10,000 a month for child-feeding, caring for some 15,000 children, as well as an appropriation of $20,000 a month for food for needy families. In all it provided help valued at about a million dollars. The Council continued its relief work in Russia only briefly after the ARA withdrew in June of 1923.

Concern for Lutheran church life in Russia continued. Lutheran congregations, and especially synodical life, languished under the harsh policies of the Communist government. In the 1920's and early 1930's they received considerable help from Americans, until still more restrictive governmental policies broke off the contacts and destroyed the synodical organization. Plans, formulated in the mid-20's for a theological seminary in Moscow to be supported and staffed by non-Russians, were never realized. On the other hand, the first General Synod of the pan-Russian Evangelical Lutheran Church met in 1924. It elected as bishops, the Reverend Theophil Meyer, who became superintendent, and the Reverend Arthur Malmgren, who headed its new theological seminary in Leningrad. A church that flourished and grew in the 1920's was dispersed and suppressed in the 1930's, going underground, though not out of existence.

Germany, meanwhile, continued to need special help. In the winter of 1923-1924 drastic currency inflation, which shattered the whole economy, brought the threat of large-scale starvation, stirring up a renewed drive by the NLC for physical relief for that beleaguered land. Though there were other special drives for emergency situations, by the mid-20's it was clear that the greatest days of postwar aid were past, because the need was not so pressing and because the wellsprings of giving had pretty well dried up. In Germany, for example, the NLC officially closed out its work in 1926. As was stated earlier, total gifts approached six and three-quarter millions of dollars by 1925. In cash and food France had received $115,000, Poland $305,000, Germany $870,-000, and Russia $370,000.

This account of NLC relief work in Europe has reflected the sequence of major emphases in four lands. Help was also given to the Baltic states and Finland. In addition, throughout the 1920's and into the 1930's, steady but not sizeable aid was given to various "diaspora" Lutheran churches. These were minority Lutheran groups (mostly of German emigrants) in southern and eastern Europe, the main assistance going to Austria, Czechoslovakia, Hungary, and Romania. By 1925 gifts for these four lands totaled more than $300,000. Space permits describing the work in only one of these lands.

Romania

A summary of contacts with Romania will illustrate this aspect of the Council's work.[2] An atmosphere of military conquest and political bitterness was the setting for the Lutheran churches of Romania in the 1920's. Most of that country's 400,000 Lutherans lived in Transylvania, a territory that had belonged to Austria-Hungary before the war. Others lived in portions newly incorporated from Russia. The change of government brought political ill-will, economic hardship, and persistent charges of religious persecution.

It was March of 1920 before Morehead reached Bucharest. After a six-day wait for a military pass, and after being temporarily apprehended as a spy near Brasso, he succeeded—as the first

Protestant American—in meeting with representatives of the three major groups of Transylvanian Protestants—Hungarian Lutherans, Saxon Lutherans, and the Hungarian Reformed. He provided $5,000 for the immediate needs of the small and scattered Seniorat of Hungarian Lutherans in Transylvania and delivered $10,000 from the Federal Council of Churches in America to the Reformed Church. He began his efforts, which were to continue for more than a decade, to encourage the formation of a united Lutheran church in Romania under the leadership of the well-organized church of the Siebenbürger (Saxon) Lutherans.

In June of 1920 Pastor Berthold Buchalla and Dr. Fritz Krauss of Hermannstadt in Transylvania came to the United States to raise relief funds for Transylvanian Lutherans from the Siebenbürgers in America. They were quite successful, raising $14,000 in several months, mainly from groups in Ohio. By the end of the year some $30,000 from such sources had been forwarded through the National Lutheran Council to the Siebenbürgers in Romania.

On September 17 Lauritz Larsen reached Bucharest. His diary relates how oriental this part of Europe seemed to him. He sought but failed to receive an interview with the Queen. After an unpleasant train trip he reached Hermannstadt on the 19th. He found Transylvania superior to the rest of Romania in cleanliness and culture. In the following days he made the acquaintance and enjoyed the hospitality of a number of Transylvanian Lutherans, particularly the leaders of the Siebenbürger church. Because of that church's dire financial straits he made a gift from the NLC of the sum of $20,000 for emergency relief and put it into the hands of a committee consisting of Bishop Dr. Friedrich Teutsch, Kurator Friedrich Walbaum, Dr. Max Tschurl, and Pastor Buchalla. Leaving from Bucharest by train on the 28th, Larsen was able to write from Vienna on October 2: "Yesterday afternoon I returned from Romania more dead than alive from the strenuous trip and the exciting experiences."

The following summer (1921) European Commissioner Morehead again visited Transylvania and succeeded in meeting with representatives of most of the segments of Lutheranism in Romania. He was able to make a grant of $11,000 from the NLC to help the most needy of their church institutions. His report of that trip was optimistic in its evaluation of Romanian Lutheran unity as it was coming to expression in the new "Evangelical Lutheran Synod of Roumania" which was based on the Augsburg Confession and included all Lutherans except a scattering of congregations representing about 30,000 Magyars. He could not, of course, be optimistic about economic conditions or the hopes for real religious freedom for these people.

Not until six years later, in 1927, did Morehead get back to Romania. Meanwhile the Lutheran World Convention had met in 1923 at Eisenach and had formed an international executive committee for continuation, with Dr. Morehead as its head. The fifth annual meeting of this executive committee met in Budapest, October 25 to November 4, 1927. In keeping with its policy of multiplying international Lutheran contacts and its practice of "deputation work," the committee—Bishop Ludwig Ihmels, Drs. Per Pehrsson, Alfred Th. Jorgensen, and John A. Morehead—went into Romania for two days to meet with representatives of the various Lutheran groups in that land. They reached Arad, where their host was Pastor Ludovic Frint, Superintendent for the Magyar Lutheran Church. There they also met with representatives of the Siebenbürger (Saxon) Church—Kurator F. Walbaum, Pastors P. Honigsberger and B. Buchalla.

Annually through the 1920's gifts of $2,000-$5,000 were sent to Bishop Teutsch to be used for orphanages and other welfare institutions of the church. And there was steady correspondence, illustrating the problems of such international contacts. There were touching examples of efforts to get food packages to needy Romanians. Special appeals by Romanian pastors for particular causes had to be turned down. On the other hand, Morehead could occasionally do personal favors, for example, helping to place a pastor's daughter in an English home to learn the language, or using his good offices in behalf of Romanian war prisoners in West Siberia.

There were also contacts with the Romanian government. NLC leaders were actively concerned about religious freedom for minorities and participated in the American Committee on the Rights of Religious Minorities, which was much exercised about

Romania. But they refrained from public leadership because it would have linked the Lutheran church to representatives of Unitarianism, and because they did not favor American interference in Romanian internal affairs. In 1920 the Queen of Romania, Marie, wrote a note in her own hand to Morehead as "Chairman of Protestant Association of Churches of U.S.A." Its one sentence read: "Sir: The kindly assistance of the Protestants in the United States of America is deeply appreciated not only by the Protestants of Roumania who have been personally benefited but by their Queen also a Protestant whose sole interest is that of her people."

Some of the correspondence dealt with painful problems. Hungarian nationalists resisted bitterly any effort to incorporate them into the Romanian nation and culture. Hungarian Lutherans resisted all efforts to bring them into closer cooperation with the Siebenbürger Church. On the other side were harsh measures by the Romanian government aimed at the Hungarian element. Dr. Alexander Raffay, Lutheran Bishop of Hungary, saw things differently from Bishop Teutsch and his colleagues on this issue. Morehead and Larsen, who were in close association with both these bishops, were anxious to avoid any partisan action. Yet they received many separate appeals for help from Hungarian Lutherans in Romania. They wanted to help where needs were pressing, but they also wanted to aid in the creation of one unified Lutheran church in Romania. Above all, they wanted to avoid the extremely nationalistic elements that were found in nearly every minority Lutheran group. Much of their correspondence reveals an effort to be both firm and diplomatic in this tangled situation.

Larsen had to discourage the sending of Romanian pastors to America to raise money, since it was hard enough for the NLC to raise its relief budget. A complication emerged in 1921 when Bishop Teutsch suggested to the Siebenbürgers in Ohio that they organize a diocese or deanship as part of the NLC. Larsen had to point out that the NLC was not a church body and that there were enough bodies in Ohio already.

This relief work in Romania and the resulting interchurch relations could be considered typical, or at least illustrative, of the NLC's contacts with diaspora Lutheran groups in its early years.

Orphaned Missions

An even more significant facet of the NLC's overseas activities following World War I was its aid to foreign mission fields cut off from support by the exigencies of war.

From its first days the Council's officers had in mind the plight of German foreign mission fields from which the missionaries had been withdrawn and for which funds were no longer available. In March of 1919 the executive committee expressed its judgment that American Lutheran mission boards would willingly take over these "orphaned" missions where necessary or take up the slack in support and administration where that was the immediate need. A month later the same committee took three actions: (1) initiating a meeting of the foreign missions executives of all American Lutheran bodies that would participate, (2) urging that the European Commissioners get in touch with foreign missions executives on that continent to see what they were thinking and what help they could give, and (3) appropriating $1,800 for Lutherans in famine-stricken India.

Stemming from the first of the above actions were two meetings of missions executives held in July to confer and organize emergency measures. The following January (1920) this group constituted themselves as the Lutheran Foreign Missions Conference of America, adopting a constitution. Meanwhile since they were mainly from the same bodies that made up the Council, they asked the NLC to represent them before the proper authorities in Washington to express their willingness to assume responsibility for the distressed missions of the European societies. This was done in the face of the threat that these missions would cease altogether or would be taken over by other mission forces and thus be alienated from the Lutheran church. There was much debate and uncertainty concerning whether German missionaries could ever return to their fields. This involved the crucial question whether non-German control and support were temporary, or whether the shift would be permanent. As it turned out, some of the change was permanent with a number of fields becoming regular mission responsibilities of the various individual American Lutheran bodies for varying and indefinite periods.

But a number of the fields remained the joint responsibility of America's Lutherans, administered through the Lutheran Foreign Missions Conference and the National Lutheran Council. The Conference, as a gathering of missions experts, studied the problems, suggested budgets for assistance and secured missionary personnel. The Council represented American Lutherans in these matters before governments, the Versailles Peace Conference, the International Missionary Council, and the European missionary societies that were involved. It supported the World Alliance for International Friendship through the Churches in its enunciation of the principle of religious freedom as it applied to German missionaries.

The National Lutheran Council also had the responsibility to raise and disperse funds to support the jointly sponsored fields. In 1920 its appeal for one and one-half million dollars was increased by $300,000 in order to meet these needs, and this became the annual process, each time reflecting the budget suggestions of the Lutheran Foreign Missions Conference. The latter part of the decade saw the phasing out of this work. By 1925 more than half a million dollars had been contributed by American Lutherans through the Council to orphaned missions. Largest amounts were received by the Berlin, Breklum, and Finnish missions in China, the Gossner mission in India, and the Hermannsburg mission in South Africa. By areas the figures totaled as follows: Africa: $113,000; China: $253,000; India: $157,000; Japan: $12,000.

Financial figures, of course, do not really sum up the significance of this rescue work in the field of foreign missions. Far beyond statistics lie the real values in terms of the preservation of Lutheran strength in Asia and Africa, the multiplying of brotherly contacts among Lutherans of America, Europe, and these lands, and, above all, the incalculable contribution to the furtherance of the Gospel.

The Nature of Their Tasks

Tasks of the European Commissioners of the NLC during this whole early period were guided by certain overarching principles. Two main ones were aptly summarized by the Commission itself in 1919 as follows: [3]

—The non-political, churchly, and spiritual character of this Mission of the National Lutheran Council shall ever be kept clear in the minds of the people of every nation.

—The aim of the Commission shall be to strengthen the position of the Evangelical Lutheran Church in each country in the matter of orthodoxy, in the unification of forces, and in its proper standing with the legitimate governments.

At times Morehead had to be quite circumspect and at other times quite firm in order to avoid entanglement on one side or the other of a bitter clash of national feelings. When told that the Americans sought to avoid the political issues, one Hungarian Lutheran commented that such a mission was "quite impractical and impossible, for politics is one of the formative elements of the atmosphere in which we all live in Europe." [4]

In carrying out their mandate the Commissioners developed certain operating policies. They tried to inform themselves about local conditions as rapidly as possible. They went as directly as possible to the responsible Lutheran leaders of any stricken area. They worked through national and local committees of Lutherans, either the officers of a given church body or a committee formed for this special service. In Germany, for instance, the director of the Leipzig Missionary Society, Dr. C. Paul, headed up such an NLC auxiliary committee for the whole nation throughout these years. For the most part, local personnel—deaconesses, church social workers, and the like—distributed gifts of food and clothing. This method was economical and efficient; it also contributed to the morale of the churches. Self-help was encouraged in every way possible.

Forced by conditions to concentrate at first on physical aid, Commissioners started by providing support to keep institutions of mercy operating. Nearly half of the expenditures, however, provided semi-annual assistance to retired pastors, widows, orphans, and others who were helpless in the emergency. At some places, notably in Russia, whole villages were provided with food and clothing supplements. In such situations there was no effort to serve only Lutherans.

Nonetheless, "spiritual" or more specifically religious aid was not overlooked. A number of unaffiliated Lutheran congregations were subsidized directly. Many active pastors were given help in order to remain at their jobs. Bibles, church publications, and other materials for worship and education were provided or subsidized. In a few cases—in France, Latvia, and Poland—money was provided to rebuild buildings, but this was exceptional.

Though they worked on a Lutheran-to-Lutheran basis, the Commissioners inevitably became involved in relations with many other agencies. They were careful to keep on good, often personal, relations with government officials, wherever they went, and frequently cultivated and used contacts through Washington or the American embassy in a given country. Both Morehead and Larsen evidenced real skill at this kind of diplomacy. Cordial relations with Herbert Hoover and the American Relief Administration were an outstanding example that proved exceedingly valuable as the only access to Russia and as a ready source of easily-purchased foodstuffs throughout Europe.

On the other hand, the Lutheran Commissioners remained friendly only from a distance in their contacts with other relief agencies, whether denominational or secular. Thus, for instance, they refused an opportunity to return to relief work in Russia in 1925 which would have tied them to a Mennonite agency, and they turned down a request for funds made by famous anthropologist Franz Boas in behalf of an organization aiding libraries of science and art in Europe. In fact, they had to turn down numerous appeals that were worthy but diverting for NLC purposes.

Morehead kept in touch with Adolf Keller, executive of the Central Bureau for Relief of the Evangelical Churches of Europe, but functioned largely apart from that organization. Similarly NLC representatives were ambivalent toward the American Federal Council of Churches in its European program. Its executive, Charles Macfarland, was unhappy that they tried to keep French Lutherans out of a church federation in that country, and American Lutherans in turn were afraid Macfarland would lead many of Europe's Lutherans away from confessional ties. Yet the leaders of these two organizations maintained cordial relationships.

Not all relationships remained cordial, however. It was not possible to carry out bold actions without meeting criticisms and sometimes sharp opposition. One repeated and often bitter accusation charged that NLC programs were anti-German, or at least not pro-German enough. Several of the German churchmen with whom Morehead worked persistently denounced Superintendent Bursche of Warsaw for his political activities which were deemed anti-German. Yet Bursche was Morehead's friend and central contact for Polish relief. Morehead always abjured any political sympathies in either direction, and he strongly supported Bursche's church leadership in Poland, admitting, however, that the open attacks on this prominent Polish Lutheran had materially hurt the NLC's appeals for funds.

Even more difficult to handle were the similar charges made by some prominent American Lutherans, usually men of an intense pro-German sympathy. They felt that the European Commissioners should have moved into Germany more quickly (though access was unavailable) and should have spent a larger proportion of their resources in that heartland of Lutheranism. There were many instances in which Americans were concerned for a particular institution in the German church and disgruntled because the Council did not funnel large amounts of money into it. NLC negotiations in the transfer of a particular orphaned mission to a particular American synod not only proved ticklish in relating Germans to Americans; sometimes they brought bitter complaints from another American body that felt it had been unfairly overlooked.

Naturally, some American Lutherans who had opposed the formation of the Council were critical of its overseas policies, stressing that it went beyond *res externae*, beyond its original charter, that it was "unionistic" and that it constantly overstepped its authority. The Missouri Synod *Witness* frequently made such accusations. Dr. R. H. C. Lenski, prominent Bible scholar of the Joint Synod of Ohio, who had participated in the first meeting of the Joint Committee on Doctrine and Practice, repeatedly criticized the Council and its overseas program in his writings.

But the most unfortunate rupture of relationships was with the Iowa Synod. In 1920 it abruptly withdrew from the Council. Though there were continued negotiations, Iowa did not rejoin until 1930 when it became a part of the new American Lutheran Church. In the first year of the Council Iowa had been a vigorous partner. But she wanted strict adherence to *res externae* for the Council. Other factors played a part—the surfacing of theological differences, Iowa's questioning of the confessional Lutheranism of the ULCA and her fear of ULCA influence at NLC headquarters. Later (1922) there was friction when Iowa Synod leaders felt the NLC had helped the ULCA take over a mission field in South America which should have been assigned to their synod. But the major field of controversy was the work of the European Commissioners.

The famed theologian, Dr. Michael Reu, led in the Iowa Synod criticisms of NLC policy, especially through the pages of the *Kirchliche Zeitschrift* which he edited. Outstanding as a scholar and well versed in German church life, Reu wielded wide influence. His strong pro-German sympathy and his antipathy to churchmen with a liberal theology soon made him a persistent critic of the more broadly conceived programs of the European Commissioners. He felt the Council was supporting the wrong groups. Like Lenski, Reu at first took part in the NLC. He had just attacked the Lutheran church of France and the work of the Council in his magazine, when he appeared at an executive committee meeting the following month (December 1919), taking President Richter's place. At the committee's request he both spoke and read a statement explaining what he had written. But such efforts at *rapprochement* eventually failed. Reu then became a critic and the chief European representative for the independent relief program of the Iowa Synod. Under these circumstances it was not possible to avoid mutual irritation in the following months of relief and reconstruction efforts. Fortunately, the Iowa Synod was able to cooperate in the momentous inter-Lutheran developments described in the next paragraphs.

Lutheran World Convention

The idea of an organization for world Lutheranism was an appropriate one for an ecumenical era. And it was natural for European Commissioners from America, establishing contacts with many Lutheran groups and forming friendships within them, to seek ways of providing enduring channels for such international Lutheran associations. Thus on John Morehead's initiative the Commissioners, meeting in Berlin in the summer of 1919, recommended to the NLC that it consider "the thought of taking steps toward the formation of a Lutheran world federation." [5]

Nonetheless, it took four years and much work to bring the first worldwide Lutheran conference, the Lutheran World Convention assembled at Eisenach, Germany, in 1923. And it took nearly twenty-five more years—and another great war—before the Lutheran World Federation was born (1947).

Lutherans had gathered in international assemblies before. For fifty years the General Evangelical Lutheran Conference had met every few years for discussions, bringing together mainly representatives from the various Lutheran bodies in Germany, though Scandinavians also participated, and sometimes men from the General Council in the United States attended. A smaller and more conservative Lutheran League was organized in 1907 for similar gatherings of men with a stricter Lutheran outlook.

World War had interrupted these contacts. Now, out of post-war distress and emergency needs American Lutherans were suggesting that Lutherans assemble on a still broader, indeed a worldwide, basis. And, since the initiating agency was not a deliberative body but an organization for practical service, it was suggested that the meetings include practical topics of inter-church aid and means for mutual strengthening in the faith.

Even in the fall of 1918 the men who were forming the National Lutheran Council gave evidence that they envisioned broad international Lutheran relationships. They spoke of establishing permanent associations with the Lutheran church in France.

Their plans for overseas work were described in the minutes under the heading of "International Lutheran Relations." They exhorted one another to permit the Council to serve as the organization through which America's Lutherans would exert "world leadership," and asserted that there is "great need of the proper understanding between the Lutheran churches of the world." [6]

The National Lutheran Council was open, then, to its Commissioners' suggestion that consideration be given to a world gathering of Lutherans. At its annual meeting in December of 1919 the Council took action on the Berlin recommendation.

It changed the word "federation" to "conference"—a considerable toning down of a bold suggestion—and referred it to a committee consisting of President Stub, M. Reu, and C. M. Jacobs. After the European Commission had again petitioned the Council at its December 1920 meeting, a five-man committee, chaired by Jacobs, got busy with plans. When Morehead had discussed the idea with German leaders, the committee met with him in April 1921 and drew up specific plans for an international meeting in the summer of 1922, preferably at the Hague.[7] These plans were adopted by the Council the following month and referred to Morehead for implementation in conference with European groups.

Topics suggested for discussion at the international gathering included: the confessions, methods and principles of church organization, the attitude of the Lutheran church to proposals of union with other churches, and foreign mission problems. Each of these was aimed at developing world Lutheranism into a more cohesive force over against other religious groups and such "isms" as Communism and secularism. Morehead stressed the urgency of holding such a conference as soon as possible since the Roman Church was very aggressive and since some European churches were unwisely trying to establish a monarchial form of government in a political context of pure democracy. He pointed out that Dr. Ludwig Ihmels, Bishop of Saxony and leader of the German General Conference, was anxious for this meeting and that Ihmels credited American Lutherans with teaching Europeans to think in terms of a Lutheran church of the world. At another time Morehead gave an additional reason for holding this gathering soon: Lutherans needed a kind of peace-making, adjudicating body (comparable to the World Court at the Hague) so that nationalistic or ethnic-inspired frictions among Lutherans would not lead to bitterness or necessitate adjudication by the interdenominational World Alliance for Friendship through the Churches.[8]

These American plans were modified at a joint committee meeting in Europe with representatives of the General Conference. Then these two bodies—American Council and European Conference—jointly issued invitations to all Lutheran churches for the meeting at Eisenach in Germany (since Germans could not leave their own soil at this time) in 1923.

One hundred and fifty-one delegates were present from twenty-two countries for the first meeting of the Lutheran World Convention at Eisenach, August 19-26, 1923. The number was kept small to provide for free and personal interchange, though thousands of visitors were present. Lutheran unity found concrete expression throughout the discussions and festivities of that week. Bishop Ihmels presided. From America there were seventeen delegates representing all the general bodies except those of the Synodical Conference. American delegates not only took part in the lecturing and the discussions, they were also active in drawing up the brief doctrinal statement and other arrangements for organization which gave the Lutheran World Convention some continuity between its great gatherings. There were clear parallels between the statement of functions of the executive committee of the Lutheran World Convention[9] and the list of purposes set forth in the regulations of the National Lutheran Council. For the remainder of their existence these two organizations were to be intimately interrelated. From 1923 to 1930 this intertwining was personified in John Morehead who was the chief executive for both of them.

John A. Morehead

From the start in 1919 John A. Morehead also personified the National Lutheran Council's work in Europe. The measure of its success—and it was highly successful within the limits of its resources—is to some extent the measure of this man. Furthermore, Morehead personified more than any other person the growing consciousness among Lutherans that they constituted a worldwide fellowship. At Eisenach his statement: "We want to help one another" struck a responsive chord among those assembled. To further that conviction among Lutherans across the globe was Morehead's purpose throughout the seventeen years until his death in 1936.

His work in Europe was grueling, especially in the earlier years. Leaving the settled tasks as President of Roanoke College in Virginia at considerable personal sacrifice—in money, comforts, family contacts, and intimate associates—he took to the uncertain railroads and highways of postwar Europe in an exhausting and lonely pilgrimage, weaving ties of mutual aid for Lutherans across the face of a continent. Lengthy letters, written by hand on shaky trains or in hotel rooms, describe how his mind ceaselessly ranged from the immediate need for shoes or food packages at his present locale to the largest issues which were perplexing Lutheran churchmen in a new age. His health broke down several times and became increasingly precarious as the years passed.

At the same time he became well known and well loved in many circles in Europe, both because he carried help for many people and because of his personal qualities. He was endlessly sympathetic toward the individuals and groups whose needs were paraded before him. But he also had a quiet strength that communicated itself readily. Not notable for his skill at administrative detail, he was able to gain the respect and friendship of people in prominent positions, could lead men and forge a hardworking team, and kept his idealism unimpaired. Herbert Hoover once said of him: "Dr. Morehead was a man of great character, devotion, and idealism. I had a most valued association with him in various relief activities after the war." Known to several heads of state and granted honors in many lands, he died while a movement was underway to secure for him the Nobel Peace Prize.[10]

Morehead's greatest contribution lay in his ability as a church statesman. He could keep a goal steadily in view and yet remain flexible and diplomatic in leading people toward that goal. In avoiding the offense of American domination it was an act of wise strategy to shift the machinery as rapidly as possible from an American operation in Europe (a Commission of the National Lutheran Council) to a Lutheran World Convention in which he was first chairman of the executive committee and then (1929) president. He did not, of course, deserve the term "Pope" of Lutheranism, given him by a New York newspaper. But when his innate fairness was under harsh attack he could resist with great firmness. Such was the case when one German member of the Convention's executive committee, Dr. Wilhelm von Pechmann of Munich, persistently and bitterly attacked him for not sufficiently promoting German causes. Eventually he stoutly stood his ground.

That the first president of the Lutheran World Convention was fair—within his clear commitment to conservative Lutheranism—and that he was eminently fit for international leadership becomes evident from the responsibilities accorded him by his brethren and the success with which he pioneered in cooperative Lutheranism at home and abroad.

A Far-Reaching Work

In summary, one can evaluate this dramatic overseas role of American Lutherans from two perspectives: what was accomplished on a world front and what it meant for the cooperative movement in America.

Writing to Lauritz Larsen in 1919 Morehead declared: "It is my personal judgment that the American Lutheran Church has never before undertaken so important and far-reaching a work as this mission to Europe to help rebuild spiritually and materially . . . . " [11] His report to the Council in May of 1921 included a section on "The Meaning of the Work" which spells out its importance.

> Perhaps the main motive at first was a merciful and loving ministry on the basis of ascertained facts to the dire needs of fellow-believers who are hungry and naked and imprisoned in impossible conditions. This supplying of physical needs

has indeed been the first and chief work of the Council but it has also proven to be a method for the ultimate accomplishment of other far-reaching results.

Morehead then turned to these larger consequences, asserting that

. . . in every country of Europe affected by the war the service of the Council has greatly helped in the preservation of our Lutheran fellow-believers as an organized force. . . . And, if it is a work of rescue of the Church of the Reformation in Europe, it is also a contribution to the salvage of European civilization, for the Christian Church in the constructive and formative forces of western civilization.

After reference to the tasks with orphaned missions Morehead summarized with this peroration:

To safeguard the Christian civilization of America; to share in the rescue of the Church of our faith and the Christian civilization of Europe; to promote the consciousness of a common work among the Lutheran forces of the world (whether in organized effort or not is not so important) against materialistic unbelief, the unrighteous competition of fellow-Protestants and the ominous aggressions of Rome; to preserve and develop as far as in us lies the resources of the Lutheran Church in the world for the church's task of fulfilling the great commission—this means to be the larger meaning of the mission of American Lutherans to their fellow-believers in Europe after the Great War.

With an exaggeration understandable in those circumstances (he was appealing for more support), these sentences do catch the larger tides of significance with which the whole venture was invested.

But what about the implications for cooperative Lutheranism in America? Later that same year Morehead claimed: "No greater specific international vocation than this has ever come to a large group of Christians in any nation." [12] Again, without endorsing the superlative, one can say that he had caught the gist of the matter. American Lutherans responded enthusiastically to the call to specific and important international tasks. This gave them a new self-confidence.

And many of them did these tasks together through the National Lutheran Council. This gave them a new sense of unity. Here was a great surge forward for the movement of cooperative Lutheranism in America, adding vital prestige to the new Council. Without this overseas program the NLC could have expired in its infancy.

However, this dramatic overseas role also led to considerable misunderstanding about the Council's basic role within American Lutheranism itself, adding to the difficulties which the Council faced in the years following 1925.

IV

Through Thick and Thin Together (1925-1938)

For the National Lutheran Council the fourteen years between 1925 and the outbreak of World War II (1939) were a time of severe testing. The first decade of this period was one of slow but steady attrition in which the Council also faced the distinct possibility of sudden death. Then came a period of almost imperceptible progress which, nonetheless, put the NLC in a stronger position when emergencies arose after 1938. Its heartbeat and pulse—public relations activities for the churches—remained firm and constant throughout this period, but its other programs and its overall budget became quite thin.

Much of the reason for this lean period is to be found in the contexts within which the Council functioned, since the church's mission always takes shape between the urgency of the unchanging Gospel and the peculiar forms which any age gives to human needs. In the 1920's Americans were disillusioned by the failure of World War I as a crusade and were rather complacent about mankind's ills. Church people were not readily inclined to man new ventures in church work. In the 1930's the depression had a stunning impact causing the American people and their churches to retrench both financially and in their vision of new tasks. Isolationism was predominant during both decades. When the New Deal proposed sweeping social legislation, Lutherans were timid and slow in coming to any consensus within their church circles. Meanwhile Nazism and other European dictatorships seemed remote to Americans, even as they became increasingly uneasy about the prospects of another great war. The American people were not yet ready to recognize their deep involvement in a pluralist, collectivist, one-world age.

During these decades the ecumenical movement gathered momentum, finding expression in a series of international, interdenominational conferences which culminated in the formation of the World Council of Churches at Amsterdam in 1948. American Lutherans were quite ambivalent toward this trend. They were more concretely interested in their own trend toward cooperation and union. This movement also gathered strength in the period between the wars. And it multiplied its instruments so that the NLC—with its limited mandate—scarcely provided the main channel for its momentum during this period. The NLC story, therefore, can be told in terms of that organization's relation to other agencies of the movement for cooperative Lutheranism. The question is: What image and role did the Council have within the movement for cooperative Lutheranism? It can best be answered by placing the Council over against the Lutheran World Convention, the American Lutheran Conference, and the various informal inter-Lutheran associations. Discussion of the informal associations will constitute another chapter, since it provides a changed perspective for the whole history.

The Council and the Lutheran World Convention

By 1925 the Lutheran World Convention was becoming operative as an organization through its executive committee.[1] The previous chapter has shown how this organization emerged in large part out of the concerns and overseas program of the NLC, with John A. Morehead as the driving force for this development. In the winter of 1923 Morehead became Executive Director of the National Lutheran Council, and the following summer at Eisenach became the official leader of the Lutheran World Convention as chairman of its executive committee.

Both the development of the LWC and the distinguished leadership of Morehead were valued assets. But they tended to over-shadow the domestic program of the NLC and to obscure its image and role in American inter-Lutheran activities.

To overcome this blurring of the image, the NLC's councillors in 1922 and again in 1926 revised the statement of purposes in the Regulations, trying to underline the regular domestic role of the Council by distinguishing two categories of purposes: Regular and Emergency Work. However, many people continued to assume that the Council was merely an agency for overseas emergency relief. Thus in 1926 Nathan R. Melhorn, an editor of the *Lutheran* who had attended NLC meetings and was its close supporter, could report that the NLC

> was established to link fellow-believers together in a ministry of love so as to apply healing balm to the wounds of international conflicts. It is true the war is now past, but the wreckage of its battles and destroyings is still in evidence and the fellowship has not yet quit functioning. This is doubtless of Providence.[2]

This misconception of the Council's primary role was still wide-spread in 1931, so that its executive, Ralph Long, could declare: "Many of our pastors and interested laymen have conceived the National Lutheran Council as an agency whose primary and chief function is to administer relief. They have thought, and some have openly expressed it as their opinion, that when this service is concluded there will be no further need to maintain the Council."[3] Actually this warped view of the NLC continued through the rest of its history.

Furthermore, it must be pointed out that Morehead's vision, even during the seven years when he was the Council's chief executive, always was directed more toward the worldwide scene than toward American developments and the Council's domestic program. In 1925 in commenting on a speech he had made in New York, Morehead told his friend Lars Boe, who was President of St. Olaf College, and the other American on the executive committee of the LWC:

> I am urging as one argument for the maintenance of the agency of the Council the fact that a general American Lutheran agency such as the National Lutheran Council is

necessary for the development of the Lutheran World Convention movement. We must have a national Lutheran clearing house in America for the Lutheran World Convention movement.[4]

As a man carrying two responsibilities, Morehead's burning passion for a worldwide Lutheranism—at a time of sagging interest in world affairs—naturally limited the creativity he could bring to the Council's domestic tasks.

But the problem was larger than the limitations of one man. It was inherent in the situation for these two organizations that the NLC play a subordinate role. Each church body participated in the Convention directly, not through the NLC, yet the machinery of the NLC was used to raise the money needed. Usually about two-thirds of the Convention budget was assigned to the Americans, though this was not publicized since it would detract from the international image of the Convention. At the same time the Council's budget for its own work—raised by the church bodies themselves—was a lesser amount and steadily shrinking.

And increasingly through the 1920's the causes were less glamorous and the money more difficult to raise. Repeatedly Morehead's vision of the needs led to a request for $100,000 for Lutheran World Service for a given year when the financially-pinched machinery of the NLC was unable to raise more than half of that amount. This was hard on morale. The councillors spent many hours at NLC meetings plotting how to raise more money and exhorting each other to greater campaign efforts. In 1929 the Reverend O. C. Mees[5] was asked to serve several months as appeal director in a special effort to raise the $100,000 goal. The net result was an increase of only $4,000 over receipts of the previous year—to $50,000. In the 1930's—depression years—annual receipts for World Service dropped to less than half that amount.

Overseas Needs

Not that LWC causes were trivial or lacking in urgency. As the Germans once again picked up their missionary tasks, and at the recommendation of the Lutheran Foreign Missions Conference of America, the orphaned missions work was phased out in three years, beginning in 1927. But relief and reconstruction needs in Europe continued. Regularly there were small amounts allocated to help various of the minority churches. Student relief—particularly aimed at keeping theological students at their preparations—became a sizeable item. Sums were appropriated to support Lutheran work among Uniat Catholic Ukrainians in Galician Poland who were undergoing a mass movement into Protestantism. Some help was extended to missionaries in China who were suffering harassment by Communist "bandits."

Consistently the largest World Service budget item went for support of the Lutheran Church in Russia. Money was given for the support of needy pastors, to train lay workers and to uphold the synodical office. The largest amounts were spent to maintain the Lutheran seminary at Leningrad under Bishop Malmgren, which was dependent for its existence upon these gifts. Begun in 1924, this school was graduating fifteen in 1929 (into a church which had only eighty-four ordained ministers). Naturally Morehead placed great hope for the Russian church in this institution.

With Stalin's accession to power in 1929 all religions underwent harsh persecution by the Russian government in the 1930's. Bishop Meyer died in 1934. The seminary was closed and Bishop Malmgren deported to Berlin. In 1933 there were forty active pastors; in 1936 the number had dwindled to eight. All organized expressions of Lutheranism were ended by 1938. Churches were closed and Lutherans went underground for two decades. The LWC and the NLC considered making public protests against these repressive measures. Lutheran representatives in Washington opposed recognition of Russia by the United States.

Refugees from Russia became a concern of World Service in the 1930's with funds directed to relief of some of the attendant miseries and to aid in resettlement, Canada being one major land of settlement. Actually, the stream of refugees from many lands was to swell for the next fifteen years, and aid to refugees was to become a major facet of NLC relief work throughout its history. By the mid-1930's it was Jewish Christians fleeing the Nazi government in Germany.

One refugee project which caught the imagination of America's

Lutherans was the rescue of German-Russian refugees stranded at Harbin in Manchuria. After a concentration camp existence in Russia and escape into China late in 1931 through untold hardships, 397 Lutheran people were helpless when all Christian refugees were ordered to leave within a few months. The Lutheran World Convention came to their rescue even though the business undertaking of colonizing four hundred people was a forbidding one for church authorities. However, as Morehead put it, "from the Christian standpoint the acutely pressing problem demanding solution is the saving of human life; the rescue of fellow Christians of our own Church from untenable living conditions; the prevention of their physical, moral and spiritual deterioration and death, and their preservation to the living and serving constituency of World Lutheranism." [6] In 1932, when amounts for other World Service purposes were only a few thousand, American Lutherans gave $21,000 for the Harbin refugees, a sum matched by German contributions.

The task of relocation was massive and complex—most of the arrangements being made by Ralph Long because Morehead was sick. Approaches were made to Canada, Australia, and Paraguay before settlement arrangements were finally effected in Brazil. Close cooperation was necessary with the Mennonite Central Committee for relief work, the Nansen International Office for Refugees at Geneva, and other organizations. By July of 1932 the Harbin refugees were in Brazil, receiving parcels of land on which to settle.

When the Nazis took over Germany in 1933, it not only affected Lutheran World Service in terms of aid to refugees, but also brought back the problem of orphaned missions. Stringent regulations of overseas expenditures by the Nazi government once again effectively throttled homeland support for German mission fields. In 1935 various loans and temporary expedients were attempted in order to assist the German missionary societies. But outright emergency gifts through the LWC to the crippled fields were also required. As with the refugee work, this was the beginning of a major task for the Council's remaining years. Throughout the central decades of the twentieth century, worldwide Lutheranism has always had urgent appeals to place before potential American benefactors.

A New Executive

Meanwhile, relationships between the NLC and the LWC had changed. At the January 1930 meeting of the National Lutheran Council Morehead resigned as its Executive Director in order to devote full time to the Lutheran World Convention. At the LWC's second great gathering at Copenhagen the previous summer he had been made its first president, having been simply chairman of the executive committee heretofore. From his standpoint the machinery created to function between conferences was quite weak and needed a vigorous hand to keep the international movement going. The limitations of his own health also pointed toward giving up dual responsibilities.

Besides, Morehead had come to see that the regular, domestic program of the NLC would not flourish without the more complete attention of a fulltime executive. In his letter of resignation he declared: "For the National Lutheran Council, the work of World Service for relief and reconstruction during the past eleven years has been overshadowing, while its permanent and regular activities in the home field have correspondingly suffered." Furthermore, he asserted that the time had come "when the work waiting to be done" for American Lutheranism "makes necessary the intensive development of its home program" by the NLC. During the three following years the NLC budgeted $15,000 annually to provide office and salary for the LWC's president.

After a half year in which the Reverend Frederick H. Meyer served as interim executive, the Reverend Ralph H. Long became executive director of the National Lutheran Council in September of 1930. Coming from the post of stewardship director for the Joint Synod of Ohio, Long was to give distinguished service to his new responsibilities until his death in 1948.

The Council was greatly strengthened by thus securing a fulltime, vigorous executive, committed to the development of its homeland responsibilities. And the separation gave the NLC a clearer identity. However, the mutual interpenetration of these two organizations continued. Annual World Service appeals remained an important part of NLC life. In addition, Long also became quite involved in LWC affairs. Morehead was increasingly confined by sickness, and Long picked up many of his duties—helping resettle Harbin refugees and attending executive committee meetings of LWC, for example. At the third meeting of the LWC in Paris in 1935 Long was elected a member of the executive committee and then made assistant treasurer in charge of LWC funds in America. In this manner the NLC executive again received official LWC responsibilities. In changing form this dual role has remained part of the NLC executive's tasks, though the influence was much more indirect during the Council's last two decades.

Throughout its history the NLC's overseas involvements have always threatened to overshadow its domestic program. On the other hand, the works of worldwide mercy and statesmanship which American Lutherans have been permitted to accomplish, under God's hand, have been of such great and inestimable worth as to reflect honor and prestige upon the agency through which they were done.

Public Relations

Nonetheless, the domestic program languished in the 1920's and early 1930's. Established fields of activity were maintained and in many ways improved, though a reduced budget curtailed some services. But no significant new fields were entered; no wider opportunities presented themselves. The Lutheran bodies did not turn to the NLC for significant new programs. The Council's role was limited to cooperation in external matters and these were defined to be overseas emergency appeals and public relations on the home front.

Public relations, of course, can be very important. The record does not indicate that it was so regarded by Lutheran church officials in these decades. The operating budget for the Council at the beginning of this period (1925) was just over $30,000.

A decade later it had dropped to just over $20,000, and in 1938 it had increased once more by only a few thousand.

Tasks of representation continued about as they had during the Council's first years. In the late 1920's Lutheran objections to the new quota system for immigrants were publicized and carried to public officials by the Council, the argument being that the system is unfair to Lutheran sections of Europe and reduces their quotas by 50%. The question of a convenient way for pastors to secure communion wine during Prohibition also took NLC staff to the appropriate government officials. In the early 1930's the issues were immigrant visas and objections to United States recognition of Russia. In the late 1930's unsuccessful efforts were made to secure provision for a Lutheran ministry to the students at West Point in distinction from a general Protestant ministry. Throughout the 1930's the Council represented its participating bodies in setting up structures for the proper securing and authentication of military chaplains. Efforts were also made to coordinate and strengthen a Lutheran ministry to the new Civilian Conservation Corps camps, which put unemployed youths to work cultivating natural resources.

In the area of representation before the public it can be pointed out that from time to time steps were taken to correct articles in reference works which were disparaging to Lutherans, or, more often, inaccurate and misleading. In 1935 a new edition of Webster's Dictionary was taken to task for its definition of "Lutheran." On such occasions statistician Kieffer would suggest the wisdom of submitting the copy for his correction before it was published.

One of the interests Ralph Long brought to his work in the Council was the radio ministry. After several false starts he found an effective service for Lutherans in providing the Lutheran preachers for Columbia Broadcasting System's famous "Church of the Air." Over the years his choice of representative clergymen from all Lutheran bodies pleased the church bodies and CBS and provided an outstanding NLC service to the radio public.

Representation of Lutheranism before other church groups continued during these fifteen years in unspectacular but valuable and time-consuming ways. The Executive Director kept in touch with such organizations as the International Missionary Council, the World Alliance for International Friendship through the Churches, and the Federal Council of Churches. When this last body urged that the NLC endorse Red Cross work in famine-distressed China, the reply was to the effect that the NLC would be happy to do so when requested by the Red Cross itself. In 1925 the Pope instituted "the Feast of Our Lord Jesus Christ as King" for October 31. This was interpreted as an attack upon Reformation Day, so that the Council adopted a statement of objection and referred it to a committee for publicity and further implementation, a committee "appointed to guard the principles of the Reformation in relation to the Encyclical Letter of Pius XI." When Council officials learned in 1928 that some American Congregationalists were working to convert Lutherans in the Volga Valley of Russia, letters were sent to the appropriate congregational church officials objecting to such proselyting.

In these ways, and in others not listed here, the NLC carried out its mandate to speak for America's Lutherans in public affairs.

Publicity

Publicity services remained on a fairly even keel throughout this period. In 1926 Morehead could report from experience that "agreeable, accurate, and helpful news covering any branch of the church does not find its way into the press of the United States and Canada by accident" but is "the result of careful planning and ceaseless effort" in which the response is greater for a "united approach through a common national agency." [7] Real progress was made through refinement of services and through accumulated impact.

On the other hand, this program was curtailed rather than expanded during these fourteen years. Periodic suggestions for a forward thrust into new activities—a full-time news writer, publicity conferences, a bureau of translations, short stories or syndicated articles for church journals, news paragraphs from foreign countries—were rejected because of lack of financial resources.

Some of these suggestions were carried out at a later date. For example, regional publicity conferences were held in 1936, though suggested in 1929. And the addition of a news writer came with program expansions in a later decade.

Winfred Elson carried these duties until 1932, working only part-time in the last year because of a shrinking budget. For the next five years the publicity bureau was under the one-day-a-week direction of a New Jersey pastor, the Reverend Charles K. Fegley. Even when one considers the added help of the executive director it is amazing how much of the program was maintained with any degree of effectiveness under these circumstances. In 1938 Osborne Hauge became full-time director for publicity, signaling the close of the thinnest years for this aspect of the Council's life.

In 1925 a weekly Church Paper Bulletin was sent to 327 religious press workers, including 70 editors of Lutheran church papers. More important were the periodic releases for the secular press. Judging from the clippings received, it was estimated that in 1926 not less than 50,000 Lutheran news insertions in the secular press were the direct result of the NLC's work. By 1930 this figure had risen to well over one hundred thousand. A third area of routine accomplishment was in the provision of news services for particular synodical bodies, usually in connection with their national conventions. These three facets of publicity have been basic to the whole work of the Council throughout this period and throughout its history.

Periodically in his annual report the executive director or the news director pled for a broader interest in news dissemination as important work in propagating the Gospel, usually explicit requests that pastors be alerted to send news to the bureau promptly and to help in securing local use of the NLC releases. Efforts were also made—with limited success—to create a network of correspondents across the country, pastors with special ability and interest in facilitating the bureau's services.

Exhibits represented another facet of the Council's interests. It maintained a traveling exhibit—consisting mainly of charts and pictures which told and interpreted the story of Lutheranism —that was featured at many conventions of church groups across the country. For the Century of Progress exposition in Chicago in 1933 the NLC helped to initiate and support a special committee which maintained a notable Lutheran exhibit for that great show. Fegley enthusiastically declared that this exhibit was "the biggest, best and most comprehensively Lutheran publicity our Church in America has ever attempted and accomplished." [8] A similar service was rendered for the New York World's Fair in 1939.

Even more a staple in NLC work was promotion of the celebration of Lutheran anniversaries—mainly through the creation of committees, literature, and publicity. Anniversaries promoted during this period include: the 400th anniversaries of Luther's Catechism (1929), the Augsburg Confession (1930), and the completion of Luther's translation of the Bible (1934); the 450th anniversary of Luther's birth (1933); the 300th anniversary of the arrival of Swedes along the Delaware River (1938).

When Ralph Long became executive director he introduced (in 1931) a new feature, a house organ called the *National Lutheran,* which was a periodical bulletin or magazine that assumed increasing importance, both in publicizing the NLC's activities and in serving the broader purpose of the dissemination of information and news about the Lutheran Church. With the advertisements and financial assistance of the Lutheran Brotherhood insurance company, the *National Lutheran* was sent free of charge to pastors of the participating bodies in the 1930's.

Along with the regional publicity conferences in 1936, the *National Lutheran* was about the only significant innovation in the publicity aspect of the Council's work during these fourteen years.

Statistics and Reference

The third area of public relations—research, statistics, and reference—also increased its effectiveness during this period without being allowed to enlarge its scope. Until his sudden death in 1937 George Linn Kieffer personified this work for the NLC, with O. M. Norlie continuing to provide valuable part-time assistance with the reference library and the almanacs. A summary of Kieffer's activities for 1934 will provide concrete illustration of the services rendered in this department.

The major purpose was to provide to all inquirers accurate information on the Lutherans of America and of the world. Often information about other religious groups was also provided. Annually Kieffer prepared an article on "Trends and Events" which summarized major happenings of the past year among America's Lutherans and was used by many yearbooks and annual reference works. To make this complete he checked many periodicals in systematic fashion and sent out a questionnaire to leaders of the various parts of the Lutheran church. He also prepared bibliographies and book reviews on a host of specialized Lutheran subjects to be used by professors, feature writers, pastors, and students. He supplied historical data and specific contemporary information to newsmen and others making inquiry. He found that many inquiries involved the question of the latest development in Lutheran mergers and unity moves and, in 1934, were concerned with Luther's translation of the Bible. He kept a check on many standard reference works to keep them up to date in describing Lutherans. Numerous telephone and letter requests sought the location of particular churches or pastors, baptismal records, when and where a particular man served as a Lutheran pastor in years past, etc. In addition, Kieffer prepared obituary accounts of outstanding Lutheran leaders. He also wrote articles on Lutherans in Scandinavia in 1934 and one on the general state of religion in America. All this work was made possible and efficient by the increasingly complete collection of materials in the reference library of the National Lutheran Council.

In statistics the services were equally varied and useful. A strong contribution to the sense of oneness among America's Lutherans was the annual one-page statistical summary, which covered all Lutheran bodies, giving inclusive totals, and which was widely used in the yearbooks of the various bodies. As statistician Kieffer also provided charts and tables for the *National Lutheran* and other periodicals, and supplied the statistics on Lutheran stewardship for the United Stewardship Council's published survey. He answered many requests for varied statistical information and wrote several articles in the field. As another service he helped to carry through the program of a conference for ULCA statistical secretaries.

Kieffer was also active, both within and beyond the Lutheran church, in seeking improvement of the methods and printed forms for securing data for religious statistics. He was aggressively interested in the work of the United States Census Bureau, agitating for the inclusion of a religious question in the general census of 1930 and again, with official NLC endorsement, for its inclusion in 1940. He was influential as well in providing guidance for the census bureau in its decisions relative to a periodic census of religious bodies.

The NLC statistician received wide recognition in his field. He succeeded H. K. Carroll in 1931 as the *Christian Herald's* man to be in charge of its annual statistical report of all religious bodies in the United States. Through his interpretive articles and statistical tables in that popular journal he became nationally known. He was the organizer of the Association of Statisticians of the American Religious Bodies in 1931 and its president until his death.

In 1938 Miss Mary Boozer, who had been Kieffer's secretary for several years, took over his responsibilities. At her request the department was renamed Information and Statistics. During her six years of tenure she gave faithful service without the pioneering thrust which Kieffer had represented.

The *Lutheran World Almanac* belonged to all facets of public relations—representation, publicity, and reference-statistics. Its value as a source of information for the Lutheranism of that day continues through the decades. It has been widely used, is much quoted, and has been an effective ambassador for Lutheranism wherever references are consulted. Kieffer, who engineered this work with the help of most of the NLC staff and many others, had prepared the material for the eighth volume before his death. His passing is probably a main reason why projections of later volumes never materialized.

On the other hand, it was costly for the NLC to produce this work, so that it is more surprising that the *Almanac* reached eight editions by 1937 than it is that the series of volumes succumbed thereafter. A subsidy of $5,000 or more was required for each edition, since it did not sell in large numbers—ranging between 1500 and 3000 copies sold. Councillors spent many hours considering ways to secure money for its publication and to sell more copies. An annual became a biennial and in the 1930's was made to cover a three-year period. It is a testimony to the importance attached to this undertaking that so large a portion of a slim budget was set aside as its subsidy. In 1934 Long quoted someone else to the effect that the existence of the National Lutheran Council was justified by its production of that series of books alone.

All the activities mentioned above, which we have called the pulse and heart-beat of the National Lutheran Council program, belong to the general area of public relations. They provided the steady rhythm or basic fabric of NLC existence. Considered external matters, they were held to be the proper arena for a Lutheran agency that had no doctrinal basis and included Lutheran bodies not in official fellowship-relations with each other.

American Lutheran Conference

What about cooperative Lutheran work in missions, education, and welfare? Except on an emergency basis, these were considered areas beyond NLC competency. But, as we shall see, by the mid-1930's and under Long's aggressive leadership the NLC was branching out into new programs, some of which went beyond public relations and touched on these other fields. Meanwhile, however, the emergence of the American Lutheran Conference in 1930 as a comparable organization with the qualifications for work in missions, education, and welfare threatened to take the wind from the sails of the NLC as the vessel of cooperative Lutheranism. In fact, the Conference seriously threatened the Council's continued existence. The NLC could easily have disappeared between the Lutheran World Convention and the American Lutheran Conference. This would have been a severe setback for inter-Lutheran cooperation in America, because the Conference did not include the ULCA whose membership made up roughly one-half of the total membership of the NLC's participating bodies.

It will be remembered (see chapter two) that doctrinal discussions in 1920 brought to the surface rather deep theological differences. The disagreement frustrated H. G. Stub's hope that sufficient doctrinal basis could be asserted to permit the NLC to function in areas such as home and foreign missions. In that same year the ULCA in its Washington Declaration, governing its external relationships, adopted some of the very statements that were objectionable to many leaders of the more midwestern Lutheran synodical bodies. These events, coupled with long-standing disagreements and differences of viewpoint, caused these midwestern leaders to concentrate upon fellowship opportunities and merger negotiations that ignored or excluded the ULCA. Earlier in 1920 the Iowa Synod had withdrawn its provisional participation in the NLC. In 1925 the Danish Lutheran Church and the Buffalo Synod withdrew their participation, the latter stating as its reason that "time has shown that Council is properly equipped to handle relief funds. So we need no further representation." [9] Remaining as participants throughout the 1920's, besides the ULCA, were the Norwegian Lutheran Church, the Augustana Synod, the Joint Synod of Ohio, the United Danish Church, the Lutheran Free Church, and the Icelandic Synod. Leaders of various of these bodies multiplied their contacts and their overtures of friendship.

In 1925 a long-discussed merger of the Joint Synod of Ohio and the Iowa Synod came into the planning stage. With the Buffalo Synod joining the planning in the same year, the three bodies finally merged themselves into the American Lutheran Church in August of 1930. This church immediately sought admission to the National Lutheran Council and was welcomed by the Council's new Executive, Ralph Long (member of the new church), even before formal action at the next annual meeting. Thus the Iowa and Buffalo constituencies were returned to the NLC. The Danish Lutheran Church returned to the NLC in 1936.

Also around the year 1925 a larger coalition of midwestern bodies began to take shape.[10] It embodied Stub's idea of enough doctrinal agreement to permit inter-Lutheran cooperation in a number of essential matters. When Stub was succeeded by J. A.

Aasgaard as president of the Norwegian Lutheran Church of America and C. H. L. Schuette was succeeded by C. C. Hein as president of the Joint Synod of Ohio, the two younger men proceeded to take definite steps. At Minneapolis in November of 1925 there was developed a document called the "Minneapolis Theses," incorporating the Chicago Theses of 1919. This became the theological basis for the American Lutheran Conference, a federation formed in October of 1930 with the following membership: the American Lutheran Church, the Augustana Synod, the Lutheran Free Church, the Norwegian Lutheran Church of America, and the United Danish Lutheran Church. The conference included virtually all the participating bodies of the NLC except the ULCA, which had been pointedly excluded from the negotiations. Stipulated in the constitution were the following cooperative functions: home missions, Christian education, inner missions, student service, foreign missions, publications, and exchange of theological professors.

On the surface of it, here was an instrument with a much greater cooperative potential than the NLC, albeit with only one-half the constituency of the Council (and less than one-third of the total Lutheran forces in America). In the course of its life it provided significant opportunities for Lutherans to get to know one another across the boundaries of diverse national origins. Undoubtedly it helped to build the mutual trust which enabled four of its member bodies in 1960 to merge into a new body called The American Lutheran Church, rendering the Conference superfluous. Meanwhile the Conference's program of cooperation had developed only certain parts of its constitutional character. Main cooperative activities were an annual all-Lutheran seminar, preaching missions and youth rallies in major cities, joint appeals for the colleges and seminaries of its constituency, and a vigorous program of student service at secular universities and colleges.

Without doubt the Conference was created by Lutherans with a fairly high degree of doctrinal consensus in order to provide fellowship contacts and an agency for cooperative activities which were excluded from the NLC's program. On the other hand, the reason for this limitation on the NLC was the participation in it of the ULCA. Thus the formation of the Conference served also as a protective or defensive league against the ULCA.[11] As such it was resented by many in that body. Stated more positively, the Conference was a move to create a "middle way" between the Synodical Conference and the ULCA. In any case it presented direct competition for the NLC as a cooperative Lutheran agency.

Turning Point in Council History

The National Lutheran Council survived this extreme crisis and developed into a far larger and more comprehensive cooperative organization than the American Lutheran Conference. There are several reasons for this turn of events. A main one is that at least some of the leaders of the Conference were strong supporters of the Council and had no intention of undercutting the latter. The Reverend C. C. Hein, a chief architect of the Conference, was a consistent participant in the Council, serving as a councillor from 1918 until his death in 1937 and as NLC president the last four years. At the crucial time (1930) he led the new American Lutheran Church into Council participation, as president of the Joint Synod of Ohio and then as the first president of the new body. Throughout the years Council and Conference were often interlocking in leadership.

Furthermore, the Council in 1930 had more than a decade of experience, with staff and machinery serving efficiently for double the constituency represented by the Conference. The logic of a developing Lutheran unity favored the broader agency. Many churchmen of the so-called "middle way" valued continued ties with the ULCA, however tenuous or external. Before long, as World War II approached, emergencies were to multiply— and for these the Council was the recognized organization.

However, another and indispensable factor in Council success was Ralph H. Long. From the time when he was invited to become executive director through his first months in that post, and indeed for several years thereafter, the Council could have failed if his nerve and conviction and energetic leadership had faltered.

The threat was quite real. There were those who felt that the Council would cease within the year.

Long was well aware of the threat. In his report to the annual meeting of January 1931 he pointed out the need, now that the LWC would take charge of overseas relief work, for radical reappraisal, a new focus, and a program of services to the participating bodies here at home. "There is," he pointed out, "a sentiment abroad that the Council must develop a wider sphere of service in behalf of its constituent bodies or forfeit the right to continued existence." His own conviction was forthrightly stated:

> There is a large field of service ahead if the cooperating bodies will stand by the Council as their common agency. It would be a backward step, a real tragedy, to drop that which has been so ably begun. There is only one course to pursue and that is to move forward with a united spirit and unified purpose.

Long's report was, of course, directed to the assembled councillors among whom were most of the presidents of the participating bodies. He was asking for a pledge of support. At the end of the report he disclosed that he still held a call, issued in November, just two months after he had taken up Council duties, to become stewardship secretary of the new American Lutheran Church. Indicating that he would ordinarily quickly return such a call because of his new duties, he added these sentences:

> However, rumors have been afloat and continue to persist even now that the future of the Council is very uncertain. Misunderstandings have arisen within the past year which threaten to jeopardize the development and progress of the Council.

He ended with a question: "Shall the National Lutheran Council be continued and is it the purpose of its commissioners to develop its program more fully and prosecute its objectives vigorously?"

Here was a turning point in Council history. Long received a most emphatic endorsement of the Council's new direction and of his leadership in it, though very little money was forthcoming in these years of depression and competing programs. The decisive fact is that Long was ready to move forward vigorously and had the confidence of Lutheran leaders in his efforts.

V

The Decisive Years (1930-1938)

Even when the basic decision had been made and the Council had a mandate to go forward, the crucial question remained: What specific programs should the Council prosecute in behalf of American Lutheranism? The history of the NLC is strewn with suggestions for new programs—small or large, sensible or wild, pioneering or routine. Some were wisely ignored. A few received rapid implementation. More of them slowly matured into specific programs. Some popped up years later at a more appropriate time.

Long and his staff turned up an unusually large crop of suggestions in the early 1930's, most of which died under the harsh financial realities which starved them. In the light of the forced economies of the year 1931 there seems to be more than the usual feeling behind the opening sentence of Long's annual report: "Under the providence of God, the National Lutheran Council has been permitted to complete another year of service in behalf of the Lutheran Church." Continued functioning was itself an accomplishment. New programs had to wait for a few years.

But what *kind* of programs belonged rightfully to the Council's tasks? Long asked himself and his colleagues that question searchingly in 1930 and again in 1936. As a thoughtful second-generation leader he turned naturally to the Council's history to give him guidance. His 1937 report includes a seven-page summary of his findings. In 1938 he published "A Brief Review of Twenty Years of Service." Since in the late 1930's the Council came as close to leading a settled existence as it ever did, it is instructive for the historian to look back from that vantage point too. The question about type of programs raises the still more basic question of the Council's nature and role.

This question had been raised repeatedly before. Iowa's withdrawal in 1920 had provoked self-searching and an effort at a clarification that would bring that synod back in. In 1922 and again in 1926 the prospect of the decline of overseas relief work led to reassessment and reemphasis upon regular and domestic work. By the second decade of Council history four working principles were supposed to define its scope.

Four Working Principles

In the first place the NLC was strictly an agency for the participating bodies. It was not a federation. Nor were the churches composing it to be considered "constituents"; they were simple "participating" bodies. As an agency it existed for specific rather than general purposes. Besides, any one body could choose to participate or not to participate in each of the program elements. Changes were effected in 1922 to emphasize these points. It should be noted that the ULCA has upheld this principle as strongly as the more conservative participating bodies. Knubel chaired the committee that prepared these changes and was willing to liken the NLC to other agencies of the ULCA, such as its boards and commissions. Knubel's successor as president of the ULCA has vigorously upheld this principle.

A second principle was somewhat of an exception to the first. The Council had a general mandate to act for Lutherans in emergencies which required a united front.

A third principle, perhaps more of an assumption, was that the NLC as a mere agency with no defined doctrinal basis had no role or responsibility in the furtherance of Lutheran unity or union. After 1920 theological discussions were tacitly omitted from Council activities.

The fourth principle was that the Council's functions were limited to *res externae,* matters not affecting the essentials of the faith. In the statement of purposes adopted in September of 1918 had appeared the phrase "without prejudice to the confessional basis of any participating Body" as a modification of the Council's mandate to represent the Lutheran church to entities outside itself. In a restatement later that fall this phrase was dropped, an action to which the Iowa Synod objected. In March 1920, in a step aimed at placating and bringing back that synod, the following sentence was added to its Regulations: "The execution of these purposes will be carried on without prejudice to the confessional basis of any participating body (i.e., without dealing with matters which require confessional unity)." This now firmly accepted phrase was taken to mean a limitation of the NLC to *res externae.* During the first fifteen years this had in practice meant that only the broad field of public relations was assigned to the Council, with the overwhelming exception of emergency overseas relief.

This fourth principle, with its distinction between *res externae* and *res internae,* came under frequent criticism by Council leaders from the start. It was asserted that the use of this distinction in the Lutheran confessions does not apply to the present situation, that its application to overseas relief would make a mockery of church relief programs and that the distinction was simply untenable. Nonetheless, it remained as a rule of thumb to determine what programs would be acceptable to the councillors and the bodies they represented. For those concerned to keep the NLC on the "external" level the first principle provided adequate assurance, allowing any church to determine which programs it would support.

Executive Director Long, like his predecessors, fully intended to stay within the rules, though he also attacked the "externals" limitation as a convenient way of "forbidding almost every new enterprise the Council may suggest."[1] In his 1937 report Long was urgent in asking for enlargement of the Council's scope and program:

> The time has come to go forward. Delay and indecision will be disastrous. It is not only a question of the National Lu-

theran Council, the future of Lutheranism in America is wrapped up in this issue.

Council history, he maintained, had shown that simply to restate the purposes is not enough. "A re-examination and revision of the basic principle on which the program of the Council is erected is necessary. This involves the relationship of the participating bodies with each other."[2] One can see that Long wanted the Council to play a larger and recognized role in bringing its participating bodies closer together. Probably he would have favored making the NLC into a federation—a suggestion which found voice a decade later.

A Broadened Scope

Long failed to get the rules changed. They never did change for the NLC. Yet the broadened scope which he desired was achieved. In fact, from the perspective of later decades one can see the broadening process was well started when he was reporting in 1937. A brief review of the program innovations in the 1930's will illustrate the forces that were at work.

First it is important to note that certain suggestions that were seriously considered did not become program elements except briefly or at a later period. A study of South America was proposed, since this was a continent of concern and budding opportunity for Lutherans. In 1933 action was authorized, but never implemented, to create a National Committee on Emergency Relief Measures for the purpose of gathering and disseminating information to the churches of workable relief plans, of significant trends in the administration of relief, and to stimulate the church to undertake emergency relief projects. An expensive project for purchasing and contributing to the Library of Congress the valuable "Lucas Cranach" Bible did not get off the ground. Pastors' Institutes for practical discussions of issues in the contemporary world did not flourish as Council programs. A proposal to help a Lutheran college develop a school of social service drew the interest of Wagner College but did not come to fruition. Maintaining a film library or producing a motion picture were ideas that persisted but did not become major program thrusts at this time. These and other suggestions give evidence that Council leadership was alert to new trends and seeking new opportunities.

Several of the actual program advances of the 1930's have already been mentioned. Coordination and cultivation in the procurement of Lutheran military chaplains were not new, but they received greater attention and were expanded to include a ministry to the Civilian Conservation Corps. Securing radio preachers for the CBS "Church of the Air" program comes under the heading of public relations but was a significant extension into a new medium. Renewed services to refugees and to orphaned missions in the mid-30's were just the beginning of what was to become a greatly expanded emergency overseas program.

Another new program during this period brought two German theological works to translation and publication for American readers. In 1934 arrangements were made with Harper and Brothers to publish Adolf Köberle's *Rechtfertigung und Heiligung* as *The Quest for Holiness*. This work was an immediate publishing success and led to the publication of Hermann Sasse's *Was heisst lutherisch?* as *Here We Stand* several years later.

A thrust in the direction of stewardship education in the 1930's reflected the executive director's field of specialization before he came to the Council. It also reflected the Council's experience of the constant pinch of an inadequate budget. Besides, the early decades of the NLC were a time in which systematic money-raising became a more sophisticated and respectable procedure in churches throughout the land. On the basis of studies Kieffer had made, Long in 1933 called for "an intensive campaign of education and stimulation in behalf of stewardship in cooperation with the various stewardship committees."[3] A quite successful conference that summer was the beginning of a series of biennial stewardship conferences and other coordinating actions—resolutions looking to common emphases, a common literature, etc.—carried through under NLC auspices.

Social Trends Committee

In 1933 Long pointed out: "The changing order in things political, economic, domestic and social, makes it imperative for the church to study the new situations arising from them and plan ways and means to study them." [4] His call for extensive study of these conditions was the birth of the hard-working and influential "Church and Social Trends" committee as well as an obvious implementation of one stated purpose of the Council, namely, "to further the work . . . of the Church in the solution of common problems affecting the religious life and consciousness of the people, e.g., social, economic, and educational problems." By the following year the committee had adopted basic principles affirming the "duty of the church to shed the light of God's Word upon the social ills and moral diseases of the nation and of the world" and declaring its conviction that "the Church ought to be aroused to a greater consciousness of its social responsibility." [5] A general statement on "The Liquor Problem" in view of the repeal of Prohibition was also presented. Both the basic principles and the statement were amended and adopted by the councillors. Publicity for the statement was authorized. Progress on further studies was reported. In 1935 the councillors adopted statements on clean moving pictures and on peace and war, enlarged the Social Trends Committee, and asked the committee to collect and study the social pronouncements of the various church bodies "with a view to presenting the united testimony of Lutherans to the world." Thus the committee's work flourished and took on heightened significance as evidence that American Lutheranism was alert to its environment and newly intent upon making its united impact felt on American society.

Subjects subsequently taken up by the Social Trends Committee included: church and state, family and divorce, the Sunday question, economic and social security and the church, communism and the church, gambling, indecent literature, boys' work, functions of the church in social relations. For some of these studies the work was coordinated with a parallel commission of the American Lutheran Conference. The procedure of adoption of these reports by the councillors was abandoned but the studies were publicized and circulated—in pamphlets, study manuals, magazine articles, youth publications—as materials helpful for the guidance of pastors and Lutheran people. In 1938 a seven-paragraph statement of principles and practices on marriage and divorce was submitted by the Council "to the various cooperating bodies of the Council for consideration and action, in order to bring about, as far as possible, unity of views and practices with respect to the matter of Marriage and Divorce within the Lutheran Churches of America."

Welfare: From Survey to Department

Still more important for the ongoing history of the NLC was an inner missions survey made under Council auspices in 1935. Initiative was taken by the National Lutheran Inner Mission Conference, an annual gathering of inner mission workers from all Lutheran synods for free discussion and consultation on common interests. This Conference, meeting in Rochester in 1931, adopted a resolution, in Long's words: "to petition the National Lutheran Council to organize a department on Inner Missions for the purpose of surveying the entire field with respect to the inner mission needs and opportunities." [6]

Since nearly three hundred Lutheran homes, hospitals, and welfare agencies across the nation had emerged over many years without any coordination, and since they represented a hodgepodge of synodical and independent institutions, with overlapping services at some places while crying needs went unmet at others, and with a diversity of standards for operation, hope for improvement in the Lutheran church's ministry of mercy lay first of all in a comprehensive survey to provide full information on existing resources and circumstances. Because the Inner Mission Conference had little organization and no authority its hope for a thorough study led it to petition the NLC for help. In the same year the Commission on Inner Missions of the American Lutheran Conference asked for authority to undertake a "fact-finding survey" which should be done "in close cooperation with the National Lutheran Council." At its 1932 meeting the NLC councillors, asserting that the Inner Mission Conference could do the desired job more efficiently, promised to support a study conducted by the Conference.

But in 1932 the two petitioning Conferences renewed their request to the NLC. Long added his plea in his 1933 report. In voicing the arguments of inner mission leaders he said that

the National Lutheran Council not only by virtue of its
character as a common agency of Lutheran bodies, but also
by precedence in undertaking a great program of World Service immediately after the close of the World War, is the
logical agency to conduct the survey. The World Service
program consisted largely of the ministry of merciful relief
in behalf of those who were destitute and in dire distress,
characterizing it as an Inner Mission activity.[7]

Here was a reinterpretation of postwar overseas relief to help
usher a new program element into the NLC. The councillors
accepted the assignment and a committee began preliminary work
for the survey.

When the comprehensive survey had been carried through, in
1935, the NLC committee in charge made a careful study of the
findings before turning the results over to the Lutheran Inner
Mission Conference. Findings suggested new studies—of chaplains at federal and state hospitals and prisons, of child welfare,
of training for Lutheran social workers, of hospitals and various
types of health centers, of social legislation, etc. New opportunities for service in the inner mission field presented themselves.
The executive director was asked to take steps to line up suitable
Lutheran pastors for chaplaincies in prisons and government hospitals. Other actions seemed imperative. In 1937 the committee
(G. H. Bechtold, S. C. Michelfelder, C. O. Pederson, G. L. Kieffer,
and R. H. Long) recommended that a department be established
in the National Lutheran Council to serve as a much needed
clearing house and coordinating agency for Lutheran inner missions. After a further assist from the Lutheran Inner Mission Conference in outlining such a department's functions, and after the
Federation of Lutheran Brotherhoods of America had added its
endorsement, the department was created and called the Department of Welfare, and in 1939 a secretary was secured.

A Department of Welfare represented the first major breakthrough in program and structure for the NLC since earliest days.
It was brought into being without any formal change of rules.
Precedent was found in interpreting overseas relief as inner missions. Provision in the Regulations was found in the same purpose
under which the Social Trends Committee came, namely, "to
further the work and coordination of the activities and agencies

of the Church in the solution of common problems affecting the religious life and consciousness of the people, e.g., social, economic, and educational problems."

Transcending the Rules

To return to the question posed earlier: Beyond public relations, what kind of program lay open to Long and the NLC in the 1930's? New elements which actually developed were the coordination of a radio ministry and of stewardship education, the promotion of two German theological works, and the vigorous pursuit of studies in two major areas—social issues and inner missions. Particularly these last two represented a broadly viable method of introducing new programs for the NLC. A comprehensive survey of an area in the church's life qualified as an objective and external activity, even though the area studied involved in some respects the church's essential life, as did inner mission ministries and marriage-divorce practices, for example. If the Council became involved in subsequent efforts to coordinate and improve Lutheran services in the area surveyed, this was a logical step in which all concurred even though the formal rules of NLC operation were being strained or evaded.

Actually the formal rules were all broken in the 1930's without being abrogated—and this illustrates the Council's whole history.

The *res externae—res internae* distinction (the distinction between external and internal affairs) was manifestly violated. Choosing preachers for national radio broadcasts is a significant participation in the direct preaching of the Gospel to all varieties of Lutherans as well as to an undifferentiated public. To label stewardship education an external activity is dubious when one considers that it involves the stimulation of the free-will offerings of Christian people. Just as Morehead could not administer relief in Europe without calling it a direct expression of Christian love and accompanying it with worship helps for pastors, so Long could not study a chaotic inner mission situation without seeking to improve it through the readiest instrument, his own Council. As Lars Boe put it in 1942:

. . . the Lord has never permitted it [the NLC] to be only an agency for cooperation in external affairs. Time and again we re-wrote the constitution and regulations . . . to safeguard this line that we arbitrarily set up, only cooperation in externals, but the Lord . . . pushed us across the line every time.[8]

Everyone knew that the Council had no formal responsibility to foster Lutheran unity. In response to a petitioner in 1935 the councillors reaffirmed that "the Council is only an agency of the Church, established for certain specific purposes, and . . . these movements in the direction of unity must proceed from within the organized Church."[9] Yet it was not unusual for the councillors to declare, by resolution in 1932, that the Council "has created a bond of sympathy and understanding among the different Lutheran bodies in America that would not have come to pass, humanly speaking, if it had not been for this agency."[10] And at a later date, referring to developments in 1930 "which created certain misgivings and distrust and disturbed the cordial relations" among Lutheran bodies, Long asserted: "It is perfectly legitimate and reasonable to believe that as a medium of common interest and activity the National Lutheran Council played an important role in bringing about more favorable relations."[11] Clearly the Council was fostering Lutheran unity. The Council was alert, too, in seeking to involve Missouri Synod Lutherans in its activities, though with little success in the 1930's. The official minutes record approaches to Missourians in connection with collection of statistics, the editing of the *Almanac*, the ministry to the Civilian Conservation Corps, the ministry at West Point, the inner mission survey, and the World's Fair exhibit. Undoubtedly there were others that were not recorded. And while theological discussion may have been taboo for the NLC, sponsoring the publication of Köberle and Sasse in America was surely a program with distinct theological significance for American Lutherans.

The effort to distinguish between regular and emergency programs in order to grant broader powers to the NLC in emergencies proved in practice to be artificial and tenuous. Emergency involvements tend to stretch out into long duration. Overseas responsibilities for American Lutherans have not really disappeared since they were first recognized as an emergency in 1918. And emergency actions sometimes set precedents for regular developments, as when the participation in inner missions in the 1930's found a precedent in the overseas relief work of the 1920's.

Most important of the formal principles is the first one, namely, that the Council was simply an agency of its participating bodies and that it served specific purposes only, with each body having the privilege of withdrawing from any one of the programs of the Council. Actually, the church bodies seldom invoked this last privilege. But there can be no doubt that this principle was important for maintaining the sovereign independence of the churches involved. Yet these assertions do not accurately describe the actual life of the National Lutheran Council. In its staff, in its councillors, in those taking part in the programs there was a morale, an enthusiasm, a sense of mission that made the Council more than a mere agency for the fulfilling of certain tasks, more than a piece of the machinery of ecclesiastical bodies. It was an embodiment of a significant movement. Because Ralph Long believed in the movement for cooperative Lutheranism and in the Council's role as part of it, he threw himself into the Council's work and aggressively sought out program opportunities.

The Role of Informal Associations

How did these new programs emerge? Technically one would expect them to be introduced into their agency by representations from the participating church bodies. It did not work that way. Long and his associates looked for needs to be met. In the case of the inner mission survey they had to overcome the reluctance of the councillors by a second appeal. New circumstances (depression, social legislation, the rise of radio) presented new needs and fresh opportunities. People, Lutheran people, turned to the Council for help.

A most significant fact about the inner mission survey, from which a department emerged, was that the National Lutheran Inner Mission Conference asked the NLC to make the study. A group of people from the various synods, who were associated in a common concern for inner missions and wanted to take positive action, turned to the Council as the structure through which they could act on their concerns. Here is a factor of major importance in NLC history, because it is the most obvious instance of a familiar process in Council affairs.

In fact, these informal associations of Lutherans across synodical lines were themselves a major facet of the movement for cooperative Lutheranism. Their story would constitute another complex and lengthy history. Some of them, such as the Lutheran Foreign Missions Conference of America, consisted mainly of church executives in a particular field. Others—like the Inner Mission Conference—consisted of free attendance of any Lutherans interested in the particular field. A large proportion of these groups were organized on the national level in the first two decades of the twentieth century. The 1937 Lutheran *Almanac* lists twenty national societies, conferences, and associations under these headings: foreign missions—four; home missions—two; inner missions—five (plus twenty-four local ones); education—four; publication—three; statistics—one; men's work—one.

The National Lutheran Council was closely though informally associated with many of these. One or another of them was constantly involved in suggesting or supporting NLC programs. During the period under review, besides the inner mission survey, one can list at least these instances: the National Lutheran Editors' and Managers' Association suggested a search for short stories and development of classified news stories from Europe; the National Lutheran Educational Conference suggested a questionnaire to test the Bible knowledge of freshmen and produced one bulletin a month for the NLC news bureau releases from 1932 to 1939; the Lutheran Student Association of America raised funds to help support the Leningrad seminary; the Lutheran Foreign Missions Conference made the basic decisions for the orphaned missions work; the American Federation of Lutheran Brotherhoods, as we have seen, joined the National Lutheran Inner Mission Conference in endorsing the establishment of a welfare department in the NLC; the American Lutheran Publicity Bureau suggested one all-Lutheran exhibit at the 1939 New York World's Fair. This list is not exhaustive.

These associations provided a groundswell of support for the Council. Despite its formal limitations the NLC was an important channel and rallying-point for these groups. In fact, precisely because of the formal protections written into its Regulations and the presence of church presidents in its meetings, the Council was able to serve as the regularized, structured, staffed channel for the informal, heterogenous, fluid and grassroots expressions of Lutheran cooperation and unity. On the other hand, precisely because it was an important aspect of a widely-based movement it often acted better than its rules would have suggested.

Seasoning

In its second phase the National Lutheran Council was shriveled by a depression budget and squeezed between the Lutheran World Convention and the American Lutheran Conference. But it developed significant new programs and added a department, gained self-confidence by weathering storms, and drew strength from the movement for cooperative Lutheranism for which it became increasingly both embodiment and reliable symbol.

As it turned out, all this was preparation for larger emergencies and heavier burdens in the years immediately ahead. It was good preparation.

VI

A Ready
and Rousing
Response (1939-1945)

Between 1939 and 1941 dictatorships and war finally engulfed the American people in a global maelstrom of strife and suffering. There was less of crusade and more of grim determination in the commitment of Americans to the Allied cause in this second and far greater World War. For American Lutherans, too, there was less of crusade but a more efficient and comprehensive response than the previous effort. Lutherans were ready the second time. Their agency for an emergency, the National Lutheran Council, was prepared to channel help for pressing human needs in the face of large-scale social disruptions. In the process the Council experienced great and rapid growth during the war years (1939 to 1945).

To the NLC one could apply the "calamity theory" of progress, which holds that significant forward movements among men are called forth by the dire threat and acute distress of a great calamity. It is certainly true that the surge of emergency NLC activity in these years was a Gospel-inspired response evoked by the crisis in human affairs. Where Christians rush to meet the needs of men, there is evidence of the church.

But for the NLC's story it is better to picture the impact of World War II as the flash of lightning at midnight, which lights up the scene long enough to reveal the basic features of the landscape. What one had to search for in the 1930's was clearly revealed in the 1940's—united action for mission on the part of America's Lutherans. The movement for cooperative Lutheranism found obvious expression in heightened Council activity during the war years. Yet it had been quietly gathering force for some time, as the previous chapter has indicated.

The Department of Welfare

After eight years of gestation, a Department of Welfare came into existence just before war broke out in Europe. Quite in keeping with the beginnings of the Council itself twenty years earlier, this department was already busy at birth.

The Reverend Clarence E. Krumbholz, secretary of the new department, had been prominent in the work of both the Inner Mission Conference and the NLC during previous years. When Ralph Long noted that Krumbholz approached his tasks "in a statesmanshiplike way," his awkward phrase did aptly describe Krumbholz's work. With vision and tact, energy and administrative skill Krumbholz made an outstanding contribution to the expansion of NLC activities in the 1930's and the 1940's.

Work with refugees became an immediate departmental responsibility, since Krumbholz, previously the ULCA executive in welfare, was already the Lutheran World Convention's appointee for refugee contacts in America. By 1946 1800 refugees had been helped to adjust to the American continent, to find jobs or homes or church ties. Most of them sought American citizenship and were aided in this process also. Assistance of staff involved both detailed individual attention and broader efforts to make wise referrals and to coordinate Lutheran help. Funds for this service to "unknown and forgotten people" were provided by the Lutheran World Convention.

Studies in both Social Trends and welfare—each begun in the mid-1930's by the Council—became a major facet of the welfare department's work. The Social Trends committee was absorbed into the committee charged with supervision of the department's activities. It took up studies closely related to welfare issues, such as the effects of population trends and social security legislation.

Soon it ceased to have separate existence. Welfare trends, on the other hand, continued to be a major concern of the department and its secretary. In 1943, for example, Krumbholz gave a perceptive summary of five trends within Lutheran welfare work itself: (1) growing consciousness of a need to coordinate our agencies and institutions in a given area; (2) marked increase in the demand for well trained and highly skilled staff people; (3) a movement by agencies only peripherally Lutheran toward closer association with the organized church; (4) a shift in emphasis from "relief" to "service," involving more specialized services; (5) need for welfare services in the war industry areas of our country. These developments were kept within the context of wider "trends" such as population mobility, increased social legislation, and growing specialization in social work.

The Department of Welfare also took over the work of the National Lutheran Inner Mission Conference, planning a national gathering biennially and arranging for regional meetings on alternate years. The promotion of this Conference (now called Lutheran Welfare Conference), preparation of the program, gathering of membership dues, editing of the proceedings, etc., constituted a major contribution of the Council to Lutheran welfare people.

In a structural change which anticipated the whole Council's structure after reorganization in 1945, the welfare department was provided with its own departmental committee that met periodically during the year to help the secretary in policy decisions, its membership made up of Welfare Conference appointees, NLC councillors, and/or representatives of the participating bodies. As the Council's work expanded and diversified, this way of bringing competent supervision in particular areas of activity proved effective. In 1941 the committee defined the department's role in these words:

> This department shall be consultative and advisory in character, and shall seek to further the development of Christian welfare service through the Churches, and to bring into cooperative relationships the inner mission, charitable, and social welfare work of the cooperating bodies.[1]

Besides work with refugees and with the Welfare Conference, there were five other major phases of the department's program. Perhaps the most important of these was the work of conducting surveys for institutions or agencies that were trying to reevaluate themselves and to plan wisely for the future. As a neutral but concerned outsider the department was able to provide objective standards, point to the facts about a given agency, and give the setting and potential relationships that affected that agency's plans for service. Over the years this function of the department has proved invaluable in helping Lutheran welfare institutions to gain perspective on their tasks and to upgrade and modernize their services.

Another department activity was its placement service, keeping a file of individual applications and a file of positions available— for executives, case workers, institutional supervisors, and settlement house leaders. The department did not, of course, do the hiring but provided full information and made referrals when requested. A more aggressive role in securing professionally trained workers for welfare agencies was taken by the department's recruitment and training program. This program included surveys, visits to colleges, counseling with students, disseminating a pamphlet called "Thinking About Social Work?" etc.

Field work visitations provided another major activity for the department. In 1941 Secretary Krumbholz spent an aggregate of four months in field visits in 80 communities, to 89 welfare organizations, including 293 conferences with workers, boards, and committees. Thus he was able to be helpful in facing a wide variety of problems throughout the land. Similarly, his department was involved in interpreting Lutheran welfare work through speeches, articles, and statistical summaries, as well as representing Lutherans in a number of national welfare programs and before various governmental agencies. To indicate the size of the field within which the department operated, the following statistics about Lutheran welfare institutions as a whole are instructive: including the Missouri Synod, there were 461 benevolent organizations (in 1945), contacting more than a million people with services, spending 16½ million dollars, involving more than 18,000 people as employees, board members, and volunteers.

Growth of the department was rapid. By 1946 there were three full-time consultants at work, a placement secretary, and three office personnel, besides the executive secretary. The budget of $35,000 was larger than the total for the Council had been less than fifteen years earlier.

Even more significant from the standpoint of changed Council policy was the welfare department's considerable role in initiating new tasks on behalf of the Lutheran bodies. In 1940 Krumbholz announced as one of three lines for future department work "extension of the task," including "organizing uncovered areas of need." More specifically, the department was aggressive and successful in implementing the first of its formally assigned activities, namely, "promotion of the organization of Lutheran welfare agencies, according to states or regions." [2] On occasion it also played a major part in the creation or the reshaping of a local agency, thus carrying the Council's programs onto the grassroots level to an unusual degree.

In addition, the department functioned as forerunner for a number of Council activities which were later structured outside the department itself. Krumbholz participated in the survey which preceded organized Lutheran services to military personnel. Under the mandate to develop "Lutheran service to special groups" and from its study of trends, the department called to the Council's attention such areas of concern as new communities near defense industries and neglected Indian groups—which mandate and areas of concern soon became part of the assignment of a Commission on American Missions. Spiritual care for prisoners of war and preparation for overseas relief programs at the war's end were two early and continuing concerns of the department.

Clearly, the Department of Welfare in these war years represented one of the great creative thrusts in the whole history of the National Lutheran Council.

Wartime Service Commission

Equally important for evidence of new life in the Council were the Service Commission and the Commission on American Missions, though these two programs were not so dramatically new because there were World War I precedents.

The Service Commission, following the men and women in the armed forces, naturally developed along lines comparable to the National Lutheran Commission for Soldiers' and Sailors' Welfare of World War I. Virtually the same title was suggested at first. Its tasks also represented continuity with previous decades in chaplaincy recruitment and authentication. This responsibility became more pressing as soon as conscription went into effect in 1940.

That the Commission's work belonged to the National Lutheran Council was clear, since it was obviously a response to an emergency and involved many relationships with the government. This program was popular because of the patriotic spirit during wartime and because every congregation and many homes had men in service. It also involved the plain duty to care for our own youth. Raising money for this project was relatively easy. Carried through with a high degree of competence and effectiveness, the wartime services of this commission were a large undertaking that reflected credit upon the National Lutheran Council, building its prestige and forwarding inter-Lutheran good will, even as it carried its ministries all over the world to serve the American armed forces.

In December of 1940 Krumbholz and the Reverend N. M. Ylvisaker began a survey which took in 42 military camps and 48 communities adjacent to camps. After their report to the January 1941 meeting of the Council, a proposed program was put into effect almost immediately with Ylvisaker as director of the new Commission and with a one-year budget of a quarter of a million dollars which had yet to be raised. Quarters in Minneapolis were provided by the Lutheran Brotherhood insurance company and immediate funds were forwarded by the Norwegian Lutheran Church. The American Federation of Lutheran Brotherhoods offered to help in raising funds. Almost overnight and with everybody's help the Service Commission was in full operation.

A year later (January 1942) Ylvisaker reported that active Lutheran chaplains had nearly tripled in the intervening months to a total of 125 affiliated with the NLC. One of the Commission's main tasks was that of upholding the chaplains in their duties. It maintained contact with them, offered encouragement and provided supplies. These last included a kit for field services and communion as well as literature in great variety and quantity for use with military personnel. By the end of the war about 800 chaplains had been processed by the Council and had been served by its Commission.

A second major facet of the Commission's task was the establishment of service centers near major camps and in the largest cities to provide recreational and spiritual facilities for off-duty servicemen, Lutherans and all comers. In 1943 there were 56 of these. Some were quite large with as many as 50,000 attendance per month. At the King George Hotel in San Francisco about 10,000 overnight accommodations were provided each month. Besides recreation, social contacts, and refreshments these centers provided various personal services, not least of which was the counsel of a Lutheran pastor. In 1944 there were 44 full-time pastors in these centers. At that time the Commission also supported 37 parish centers or part-time service centers. Attendance for the year at these centers approached three and one half million. Hundreds of clergymen in local congregations were upheld by the Commission in similar duties where centers could not be established.

Another responsibility of the Commission was the more general one of encouraging local congregations to keep in touch with their servicemen, helping them to keep informed about spiritual resources, the transfer of records, etc., for the men in service. For chaplains, for service pastors, and for direct contact with military personnel the Commission produced and distributed great quantities of a variety of literature. Through 1945 Ylvisaker could report the following distribution totals for the whole period:

Tracts, devotionals, booklets, books	13,809,461
Service Prayer Books	937,900
Army and Navy Service Books	469,360
Periodicals	34,707
Publicity materials	1,166,000
News Letters	343,200
Service Men's Stationery	14,460,000
Office stationery	990,000
Christmas stationery and cards	1,000,000

Communion cards	550,000
Field Communion Kits	635
Private Communion Kits	555

With a budget of $600,000 in 1944 the Service Commission had a growth which Ralph Long characterized as "truly phenomenal." "To get a complete and well-rounded picture," Long added, "one should also have access to the many letters that are written home by service men and women concerning the value of this ministry. . . . Only God knows how far-reaching and effectual this ministry has been." [3] The Commission's work compared favorably with similar programs by other denominations, and, indeed, at several points provided patterns and materials used by other groups.

By 1945 emphasis turned to demobilization and the successful return of servicemen to home communities and churches. Though the program slackened, it was obvious that a sizeable spiritual ministry in the armed forces would continue for some time. Thus a temporary Commission was transformed into a permanent Bureau of Service to Military Personnel in 1948.

Because of the intermingling of Lutherans which military service involves, the Service Commission played a significant role in promoting inter-Lutheran understanding and good will. As in World War I, a degree of cooperation with the Missouri Synod was developed. It was held to be cooperation in externals and involved mainly joint planning in the location of service centers and joint support and provision of pastoral services at most of the centers. Such coordination included the understanding that "spiritual welfare work in the interest of members of the Missouri Synod" would be done by Missouri Synod pastors and that the same would be true for the NLC. In this wartime emergency informal cooperation between Missourians and other Lutherans marked an advance over the previous decades, though formal agreements were little changed from the World War I pattern.

American Missions

The Commission on American Missions also emerged under wartime conditions with an emergency and temporary mandate. However, its growth paralleled the Department of Welfare, rather than the Service Commission, because it developed out of an informal inter-Lutheran group, the Lutheran Home Missions Council, and because it quickly took on expanded and abiding programs that transcended the war emergency.

The new Commission was organized in the fall of 1942 to meet the needs of Lutherans in the mushrooming temporary communities formed around defense industries—a situation that paralleled the beginning of the NLC itself in 1918, though this time the scale was much greater and the duration considerably longer. After brief study by both the Home Missions Council—composed of home missions executives of the bodies—and the NLC, the executive committee of the latter acted decisively, secured $25,000 from the home missions boards of the churches, and called the Reverend H. Conrad Hoyer as the director for a Commission on American Missions. Hoyer's work was supervised by a committee composed largely of the same home missions executives, who were thereby transferring their cooperative planning and action from an informal Home Missions Council to a more formal Commission of the NLC with its own staff.

The already functioning Commission was given formal approval in January of 1943 by the Council itself and its program reached high gear by the middle of the year, with its budget of $150,000 still to be raised as part of a larger appeal. Its major task was to coordinate Lutheran ministries to large concentrations of temporary settlements caused by defense industries or other wartime dislocations. It maintained its own membership contact-and-transfer program and sought to stimulate such services by the Lutheran bodies themselves. It placed clergymen and/or women visitors in a number of strategic localities and in others it supported the special program of well-located congregations designated as Defense Industry Centers. It provided special literature, suggestions for canvassing or visitation programs, help in coordinating local committees, etc. It also functioned as the representative of Lutheranism in interdenominational, community, or governmental agencies with this particular concern.

In 1945 the Commission's staff totaled 65, including 15 pastors and 34 women workers in the field. Reporting for the two and a half years ending in December 1945, Director Hoyer gave the following statistical summary of these activities:

Reaching — 185,000 home calls made for Christ and His Church in War Boom communities; thousands of these referred to local churches for war-time spiritual care.
800,000 pieces of Christian literature distributed to people on the move.

Teaching — 56 emergency Sunday Schools organized and conducted in War Housing communities. Weekly average attendance in these Sunday Schools during the past two years was 3,600 pupils.
10,000 children enrolled in Vacation Bible Schools.
Week day church school and Bible story hour programs in 30 temporary home communities.

Preaching — 30 emergency worship programs arranged in war-time communities, with 1,800 souls as the weekly average attendance at these services during past two years.

Ministering — 6,000 souls communed; 600 souls baptized; 4,000 sick beds visited. Many thousand home calls for personal counselling in sorrow and distress. Thousands of youth enrolled in Luther Leagues.

Of much greater significance for inter-Lutheran cooperation was the new Commission of American Missions' role in developing comity (i.e. mutual recognition) agreements among participating bodies of the NLC in the establishment of new congregations on a regular and permanent basis. Here was a more direct confrontation with a more essential aspect of denominational life than any previous area of work opened to the National Lutheran Council.

There were both exterior and interior reasons why this kind of crucial cooperation became possible at this time. The crisis of warfare put a new perspective on intramural squabbles. Tremendous movements of population—20,000,000 people changing homes in two years, and the sudden growth of great cities with the proliferation of suburbs indicated that the field of opportunity was greater than combined Lutheran resources. Increasingly each Lutheran body was doing its work in the same common tongue, English, and reaching out to the whole community, rather than merely its own ethnic group, so that competition became even more odious. Above all, people were coming to recognize that "other Lutherans are fellow Lutherans," [4] so that overlapping and competition among congregations increasingly appeared as wasteful and divisive within the household of faith. Twenty-five years of the National Lutheran Council had helped to develop this viewpoint.

There had been important moves in this direction before. The Lutheran Home Missions Council of North America, organized in 1931, had as its purpose just such cooperative planning. But only in the 1940's had it reached the stage of organizing regional committees that would allocate a particular field to a particular Lutheran body for the establishment of a mission church. To the new Commission of the Council was given the mandate to implement and refine this regional machinery.

The United States was divided into twenty-six regions and in 1944 it was reported that regional home missions councils were functioning in eighteen of these. Detailed procedures were developed for constituting the membership of these councils, keeping records, guiding allocation procedures, providing methods of adjudication of disputes, etc. Probably Long was overstating the case when he asserted that "rivalry and competition have been relegated to the limbo of the past," but he was accurate in adding that "a remarkable cooperation has been achieved, for which the whole Church ought to be grateful." [5]

Since the Home Missions Council was absorbed into the Commission on American Missions, another of its main duties fell to Hoyer and staff, namely, the sponsoring of an annual conference on home missions. Two conferences were held in 1944. The one held in Canada made the serious suggestion of the formation of a Canadian counterpart to the National Lutheran Council. The one held in Minneapolis recommended that the NLC establish a department on rural church life and undertake cooperative action in behalf of minority groups. The Canadian suggestion came to fulfillment in the next decade. The other recommendations were picked up almost immediately, though the rural life program belongs to the next period of NLC history.

A cooperative ministry to minority groups had been under consideration before the Minneapolis conference. The previous year, with an eye to joint action, the Commission had begun a survey of what was being done by the participating bodies "in the fields of Jewish missions, Mexican missions, Migrant missions, Oriental missions, Colored missions, Latin American missions, Mountain missions, American Indian missions, etc." In 1945 authorization was given the Commission to launch into work with Negroes and work with Jews.

Implementation of these new program thrusts took place in the next period of the Council story. But here it is important to note that this proliferation of program in missions, assigned to a Commission that was at the same time reorganized for permanent status as a Division of the Council, reflected an expansive mood on the part of NLC leaders which caused one member of this Division to report in 1946: "Interestingly enough there seems to be no end of work for the Division to do." [6] This optimism was in striking contrast to the mood in 1936 and, as we shall see, in 1956 as well.

International Outreach

Meanwhile, the outbreak of war in Europe in 1939 brought drastic changes to world Lutheranism and the role of Americans in it. The international structure of the Lutheran World Convention was at an end for the duration and the American Section of the LWC really functioned in its behalf during war years. Naturally, plans for the fourth international conference in the United States in 1940 were dropped. The flow of refugees to North America increased. With the interning of German missionaries in Africa, the Near East, Asia, and the South Sea Islands, these mission fields, already handicapped by Nazi regulations, became orphaned missions once more. The Russian invasion of

Finland cut off support for the Finnish mission fields and created distressing needs in that Lutheran homeland itself.

American Lutherans girded themselves to provide help. They were prepared. Indeed, they had two agencies ready—the National Lutheran Council and the American Section of the Lutheran World Convention. In theory these were separate organizations because the American participating bodies in the LWC had direct representation instead of using the NLC as their agency to approach world Lutheranism. In actuality the NLC and the American Section of LWC were closely interlocking. A 1941 statement adopted by the NLC asserted that these two agencies may be said to be coextensive since they serve the same Lutheran bodies and that the NLC is to carry out the practical work of the American Section—such as publicity and appeals for funds, though the Council cannot take over the American Section's responsibility to represent American Lutherans within world Lutheranism. At the same time an agreement was reached with the Missouri Synod for a coordination of efforts in the support of orphaned missions.

Lutheran World Action was the name given to the gifts of money by American Lutherans poured out in response to a war-torn and deeply distressed world. In a sense Lutheran World Action was also the worldwide program made possible by these gifts, carried out by various departments of the NLC, by the agencies of world Lutheranism, and by various ecumenical projects of mercy and mission.[7] Besides, Lutheran World Action, as an appeal, a phrase, and a stirring idea, together with its symbol of a strong arm thrusting the cross forward (Love's Working Arm), has been one of the great accomplishments of the National Lutheran Council, sustained throughout the last 25 years of its history.

The phrase was coined for the NLC's appeal for emergency funds in the fall of 1940. A previous Lutheran Emergency Appeal, primarily for orphaned missions and directed by the veteran O. C. Mees, had produced $238,000 by the spring of 1940. The new appeal for half a million dollars was named Lutheran World Action. Under the direction of Long the Reverend Paul C. Empie assisted in the preparation of literature, involving about six pieces totaling nearly two million copies, and in the development of an organization that included about forty regional directors. Once again the Council had embarked on large-scale fund-raising based on a direct appeal to millions of Lutherans in America on behalf of orphaned missions, refugees, and men and women in the armed services.

Receipts during 1939-1941 totaled $844,000. Thereafter, annual appeals were met by increased giving. In 1943 the goal of one million dollars was exceeded by more than $300,000 and the councillors faced the strange task of allocating surplus funds. In 1944 $100,000 was designated for postwar European relief and rehabilitation. The budget for that year's appeal included these items:

Service Commission ....$	600,000
Church Abroad	
(a) Orphaned Missions	350,000
(b) European relief	100,000
Commission on American Missions	150,000
Emergency Welfare Service	25,000
Unforeseen Emergencies	17,000
War Prisoners' Aid	
(a) Y.M.C.A.	18,000
(b) Lutheran Commission	25,000
War Time Radio Ministry	10,000
American Bible Society	15,000
Refugees	5,000
	$ 1,315,000

In 1945 the item budgeted for "Church Abroad" had doubled, heralding the shift from wartime to postwar tasks. Receipts went well over the two million mark. Still larger campaigns were to come, when direct help in ravaged Europe became possible.

Prisoners of war presented a responsibility and an opportunity for America's Lutherans. In 1944 there were approximately 400,000 of them in the United States. Most of them were Germans and half the Germans were in some sense Lutheran. The National Lutheran Council entered into formal agreement with the Missouri Synod in the fall of 1943 to form the Lutheran Commission for Prisoners of War. Its tasks were to locate and authenticate

Lutheran clergymen among the prisoners, supporting them in providing a ministry for their men; to provide literature such as service books and prayer books; where possible to provide a ministry of Lutheran chaplains or clergymen to prisoner of war camps; and to foster the general welfare of the prisoners of war. This last was done largely through support of the YMCA's work.

For the NLC the Department of Welfare carried this responsibility. An executive secretary and two field secretaries were secured for this ministry, which helped to arrange worship services at numerous camps for two and a half years. More than one hundred Lutheran ministers and theological students were found among the prisoners. The work was also extended to prisoners of war in Europe through dozens of American chaplains. A staff member of the welfare department collected and dispersed 250,000 books, mainly religious, to prisoners in the United States in more than 400 camps, and more than 600,000 books for use in the prisoners' camps in Europe. By 1946 the American phase of this program was ended, but, as Executive Director Long indicated, "the spiritual blessings of this ministry are beyond computation." It also marked another milestone in formalized relations with the Lutheran Church—Missouri Synod.

Moves Toward Lutheran Unity

In the 1940's the NLC became involved in moves toward Lutheran unity in a way that would have been impossible a decade earlier.[8] This reflected a new confidence which Lutherans as a whole were placing in the Council. It also reflected a new friendliness among America's Lutherans, and, above all, a deep awareness that "the present desperate crisis in world affairs" was challenging American Lutherans to close ranks in order to meet the problems.

This last reason was the one stressed by a group of Lutheran editors in appealing to the Council at its annual meeting in 1942 to study "the feasibility of setting up an All-Lutheran federation which could make use of the National Lutheran Council as its working agency." The councillors responded by adopting unanimously with a rising vote a resolution which asserted that the

Council believed "that the time has now come for closer cooperation among all Lutheran bodies in America in a Lutheran federation." The resolution concluded with the prayer that

> such a federation may constitute a step toward that ultimate
> unity of American Lutheranism demanded by the challenge
> of the future, and so deeply desired and so longed for by
> many . . . in all our general bodies.[9]

A special committee, including the synod presidents, met in
March and in May to consider plans for a federation, along with
other matters. They proposed, after considerable discussion of
the alternatives, enlargement of the American Lutheran Conference "so that its constituency may become representative of
the Lutheran Church in America." [10] Meanwhile, they further
proposed, let the NLC sponsor from time to time free general
conferences to discuss mutual opportunities for service, and let
the Council itself look toward expansion of its services. Presidents of non-Council bodies were invited to the May meeting in
Columbus, Ohio. President John W. Behnken of the Missouri
Synod, who had been present and had informally addressed the
councillors at the annual Council meeting of 1940, accepted this
invitation and was present with four other Missouri leaders for
one session. The Missourians affirmed their desire for Lutheran
unity based on complete doctrinal agreement, their willingness
to cooperate in purely external matters, and their disinterest in
any new structures for cooperation except as emergencies demanded them.

In 1945 a new constitution for the Council included as one
purpose: "The convening of a triennial general conference of
representatives of the Participating Bodies, for the study and discussion of practical problems common to the Lutheran churches
in America. . . ." In 1949 plans for holding such a conference
were dropped. No other formal steps toward Lutheran unity were
taken by the Council as such.

Reorganization

During these years real progress in inter-Lutheran relations
consisted of major expansions of NLC program, as this chapter

has documented. Reorganization of the Council itself was one major result of this growth. Reorganization was also a preparation for the further expansion which was anticipated for the postwar years.

Before 1939 the Council's major homeland work was public relations. During these seven years that activity continued in substantial but not greatly altered fashion. However, major breakthroughs came in the fields of welfare, service to military personnel, and American missions. By 1944 it was evident that student work and European relief and reconstruction would become major new programs. The agenda for annual meetings became crowded and specialized, requiring twice the time (four days in 1945). Staff increased, including an assistant to the executive director in 1944. It became the growing habit to refer many crucial decisions to the executive committee. The regular budget, apart from Lutheran World Action, increased steadily until it tripled depression budgets ($71,000 in 1946). The Regulations, last revamped in 1926, were outdated, and a full constitution was now needed. Reorganization became imperative for the sake of efficiency and proper supervision of all activity.

There were other reasons for stock-taking. The new warm-up in inter-Lutheran relations and talk of an all-Lutheran federation raised the question of the Council's continuing role. The technical matter of incorporation of the NLC was under consideration throughout these years. Since the Council's participating bodies included Canadian members, it helped in the formation of a Canadian Lutheran wartime commission. This action in 1940 raised the question of a Canadian Lutheran Council which finally came into being in 1952. Many other relationships with a variety of agencies—Lutheran, Protestant, secular—had to be rethought during wartime. In 1942 the Suomi Synod was received into the Council, bringing the number of participating bodies to eight.

Stock-taking was also spurred by the passing of the last of the first generation of NLC leaders—F. H. Knubel, L. W. Boe, J. A. O. Stub, Peter Peterson, and E. F. Eilert who had served faithfully as the first treasurer for twenty-two years. Completion of twenty-five years of Council service, coupled with Ralph Long's interest in the NLC's history, led to the 1945 publication of *Lutherans Working Together*, a small book by Osborne Hauge, giving an overview of the Council's first quarter century.[11]

Much time and planning were put into reorganizational efforts, even though other tasks pressed upon councillors and staff. Finally, in January 1945, plans came to a head in the adoption of the first formal constitution, just as councillors were being introduced to new headquarters at 231 Madison Ave., New York.[12] Most significant change from the 1926 Regulations was the expansion of the sixth purpose, which had previously mentioned only information and statistics, to read:

> To undertake and carry on such work as may be authorized by the Participating Bodies in fields where coordination or joint activity may be desirable and feasible, such as publicity, statistics, welfare work, missions, education, student work, and other fields.

This was largely recognition of areas of activity already entered. At the same time it was a listing quite similar to that describing the proposed tasks for the American Lutheran Conference in 1930.

Structural changes incorporated in the new basis for Council government provided for Divisions, Departments, Bureaus, and Commissions. A Division was defined as "a functional agency in a particular field of work"; a Department was to be a sub-section of a Division; a Bureau was "a functional agency in a limited field"; and a Commission was a functional agency serving "in a temporary or emergency situation." At that time permanent status as divisions, with their own supervisory committees, was given to public relations, welfare, and American missions. The Service Commission soon became a Bureau.

The new constitution also spelled out more explicitly steps to be taken in introducing new program elements and in other ways prepared for a future of increased usefulness. At the same time, through bylaws and other actions, administrative machinery was put into more careful order as befitting an institution that was maturing and moving into more complex operations.

Taking effect just at the time when exciting postwar opportunities were opening up for the Council, the constitution provided the necessary structure of government to undergird the new work. On the other hand, it permitted much less leeway for the kind of strong executive leadership which had characterized the Council in the first half of its life.

Unparalleled Upsurge

For the National Lutheran Council the years from 1939 to 1945 represent a tremendous and unparalleled upsurge. This is attributable to three factors: the world situation, the swelling of the movement for Lutheran cooperation and unity, and the well-earned reputation of the Council itself as the most effective channel for that movement and a trusted agency for the cooperative activities of its participating bodies. Particularly in the fields of welfare and American missions the Council had found pathways to new and significant cooperation. Whereas in the 1920's and 1930's informal inter-Lutheran associations had helped to uphold the Council's existence, now the NLC took over their roles or upheld them in their purposes. Programs which were reserved for the American Lutheran Conference in 1930, because they went beyond externals, now became an accepted part of NLC routine. In 1942 Dr. E. E. Ryden, Lutheran editor and leader in the Conference, had prophetically suggested that the Conference would become "a forum or consultative organization" while the Council would take over some of its activities and become the comprehensive working agency for cooperation.[13]

Before World War II, as Paul Empie was to point out years later, the Council program was aimed primarily at representing American Lutherans before the public or to European Lutherans, in keeping with the phrase in the Council's preamble which asserted that the participating bodies seek to serve "the Lutheran Church at large" through their cooperation. But, as Empie put it,

> with the coming of World War II, the role of the Council was strengthened substantially in the direction of that of an agency through which the bodies might coordinate or conduct jointly certain of their own activities—that is to say, work which they regard directly as their primary responsibilities

and only indirectly as serving the "Lutheran Church at large." [14]

This is the shift Ralph Long had asked for when he became executive director in 1930.

In 1946, at any rate, it was clear that the Council, as the central organization for cooperation, was strong and gathering strength.

It had even entered into negotiations to foster a larger Lutheran unity or union, a role for which it had no clear mandate. Its leaders were somewhat optimistic about a breakthrough in this direction. On the threshold of the postwar world Long noted how mutual confidence had quickened in recent years. Approaches to Lutheran unification through theological formulae had been disappointing, he felt.

> It now appears that through the process of an ever-widening cooperation in the work of the Church through the National Lutheran Council, the desired goal may ultimately be reached. [15]

That goal has not yet been reached, and Long probably did not expect that "ultimately" would extend beyond two decades, for he was enthusiastically proclaiming the dawn of a new era for the Council. However, his statement of the process which gave greatest promise of success represented a valid insight which has been verified by subsequent events. Meanwhile, the 1940's held no real breakthroughs in formal arrangements among Lutheran bodies, despite efforts by the Council and by other means.

VII

Postwar Crescendo

(1946-1952)

In December of 1946 Paul Empie visited war-devastated Europe for the first time. Later he described to the present author one vivid experience. "By far my most appalling sight of destruction was in Warsaw. Whole blocks of houses had been reduced to piles of rubble; transportation was provided by a few antique tram cars bulging with people, by 'rickshaws' which looked to me like park benches on wheels pushed by bicycles, or by horses; few houses had heat in the winter temperature, which was about five above zero, and the threadbare clothing of those seen on the streets of the city couldn't have provided much comfort or protection from the bitter winds.

"During my stay I met with leaders of the church to tell them of our plans to send additional relief in the form of food, clothing, medicines, and money. I shall never forget the comment made by a layman. I can't repeat it verbatim but the substance of it was as follows:

> Over twenty-five years ago when Poland was still suffering from the horrors of World War I, I was undernourished and ill, with little hope of survival. At that time, to my amazement and gratitude, supplies from the National Lutheran Council in America saved my life. I promised myself never to forget this and hoped that some day I could repay by helping someone else. Isn't it ironic that just about a quarter

115

of a century later Lutherans from America have to come to me and do it all over again! It's enough to make one lose faith in the intelligence and integrity of mankind; only the constant love of Christian brethren offsets despair by reminding us of the never-failing love of God.

War's Aftermath: Second Cycle

The exciting experiences of the National Lutheran Council following World War II presented striking parallels to the earliest days of the Council following World War I.

Again, but on a larger scale, devastation of life and property and dislocation of peoples and the social fabric were paralyzing for Europeans and evoked aid programs from concerned Americans. Again, desperation, cynicism, and Communism threatened to crush Christianity in many European lands. Again, Lutherans were particularly hard hit, providing a severe test of faith for European Lutherans and a severe test of generosity for American Lutherans. Once again the Council threw most of its resources and imagination into dramatic and compelling overseas challenges.

Of course, there were important differences. The need and the response were much greater and more sustained. And the Council was much better prepared this time. It had been saving money for relief and reconstruction. More important, it had had twenty-five years of experience and contacts upon which to build.

In another respect these are parallel periods for NLC history. Each was a time of ferment in inter-Lutheran relations in America. At the Council's birth there had been other evidences of a new willingness to cooperate and there were several significant mergers. Similarly, the 1940's was a period of notable increase in cooperation—as the previous chapter and the present one indicate. And Lutheran leaders rather generally felt that the time was ripe for a major advance toward Lutheran federation or union.

Lutheran Union Proposals

NLC-sponsored proposals in 1942 for a larger federation and for free conferences did not materialize during war years. But

Executive Director Long remained alertly hopeful. Less than a month before his untimely and tragic death, February 19, 1948, his assistant, Paul Empie, read to the councillors at the annual meeting the ailing Long's supplement to his regular report. It was a restatement of his belief that cooperation should continue and "must eventually lead to unity of American Lutheranism." Long noted that voices were increasingly calling for cooperation in areas heretofore reserved for the separate bodies. Typically he made his own proposal in the form of a question:

> In view of these stirrings within the Lutheran Church, I raise the question whether the churches should not now give serious consideration to a wider cooperation which would of necessity involve some form of organic union.[1]

Several similar appeals were made in that same year.[2] In a rousing plea the Lutheran Editors' Association even referred to the action of its editors at the 1942 meeting of the NLC. But the Council itself carefully refrained from any participation in union moves. In 1949 it postponed "the proposed Triennial Conference" (which was never held), and the president of the Evangelical Lutheran Church withdrew the request of his Church Council that the National Lutheran Council call an All-Lutheran Conference.

Nonetheless, the context for Council work in these years was a series of proposals which would have altered the relations of the participating bodies. In January of 1949, several weeks before the NLC annual meeting, representatives of six of the Council's bodies met as a Committee of Thirty-four on Lutheran Unity. In this committee and in other discussions there were suggestions of a broadly inclusive federation or a comprehensive merger of the eight bodies participating in the Council. By the end of this period, however, these ideas had faded as immediate possibilities; the only concrete program that was making progress was merger among the bodies of the American Lutheran Conference. Theological differences similar to those which surfaced in 1919-1920 and continuing mistrust thwarted hopes for a larger merger in the decade after World War II. One is tempted to conjecture whether the continued presence of Ralph Long, as an ardent, respected, and tactful advocate of greater Lutheran unity, would have altered these disappointing events.

In any case, further formal steps toward unity on the part of the Council had to wait for a decade and then involved more inclusive cooperation rather than comprehensive merger, quite in keeping with the whole of Council history. We turn now to the several areas of advance in cooperative activity through the NLC.

Student Services

In 1945 a Commission on Student Service was created by the Council with primary responsibility in behalf of the participating bodies for ministry to students on non-Lutheran college and university campuses. This step was not simply an expansion of Council program, though this work soon became the largest domestic division in staff and budget. It was also the most directly operational aspect of NLC work, i.e., student work was not so limited to consultative and coordinating functions as were other divisions, but was directly involved in carrying through the actual, local ministry. Equally important, student service touched more closely the essential and inner work of the churches because it involved crucial spiritual cultivation of the churches' youth, especially their potential leaders. The church's own schools enrolled only a small percentage of the Lutherans in higher education. For these reasons the student commission was an unusually significant step forward in the movement for cooperative Lutheranism.

The new Commission incorporated two thriving predecessor programs. Twenty-five years earlier the ULCA had begun its specialized student work by appointing pastors near universities as student pastors and providing national staff to develop a ministry to students. In 1938 the American Lutheran Conference had created a Student Service Commission, which, under the leadership of the Reverend Fredrik A. Schiotz, quickly became the largest operational element in the Conference's program. Schiotz worked in close concert with ULCA staff, and, at the risk of unpopularity in some circles, took the lead in securing agreement of Conference officials to the transfer of this program to the

DR. LAURITZ LARSEN
first executive secretary of the National
Lutheran Council, 1918-23.

DR. JOHN A. MOREHEAD
executive secretary of the National Lutheran Council, 1923-30.

DR. RALPH LONG
executive secretary of the National Lutheran Council, 1930-48.

DR. PAUL C. EMPIE
executive director of the National Lutheran Council, 1948-66.

DR. OSCAR MEES

interim executive secretary twice, who also served in nearly every executive position in the NLC in its early history.

DR. H. G. STUB

first president of the National Lutheran Council.

Below: Dr. George Linn Kieffer in his office as statistician and financial secretary of the council.

Above: Committee #3, "The Lutheran Church in the World," as they prepared for the first Lutheran World Convention in Eisenach in 1923. Standing, left to right: Dr. B. M. Christensen, Dr. E. E. Fischer, Dr. T. F. Gullixson, Dr. Conrad Bergendoff, Dr. E. C. Fendt. Seated, left to right: Dr. L. W. Boe, Dr. F. H. Knubel, Dr. W. H. Greever, Dr. Ralph H. Long.

Below: Presidents of the eight participating churches of the NLC at the annual meeting in Richmond, Va., in 1948. Seated, left to right: Dr. T. O. Burntvedt, Lutheran Free Church; Dr. Em. Poppen, American Lutheran Church; Dr. P. O. Bersell, Augustana Synod; Dr. A. Haapanen, Finnish Suomi Synod. Standing, left to right: Dr. J. A. Aasgaard, Evangelical Lutheran Church; Dr. Franklin Clark Fry, United Lutheran Church in America; the Rev. Alfred Jensen, Danish Lutheran Church; Dr. N. C. Carlsen, United Evangelical Lutheran Church.

Above: Prof. M. J. Stolee, commissioner, Dr. Lauritz Larsen, executive secretary, and Dr. John A. Morehead, chairman of commission, met in Berlin in 1920 to plan the course of National Lutheran Council reconstruction in Europe.

Below: Research in the early days: Dr. Ralph Long, executive secretary of the council; Dr. E. B. Burgess, president; Dr. George Linn Kieffer, secretary of statistics and research.

Right: Dr. Paul C. Empie, executive director of the NLC, and Bishop Hanns Lilje, president of the Lutheran World Federation (1954).

Below: Dr. Paul C. Empie, executive director of the National Lutheran Council, confers with Dr. W. A. Mehlenbacher (left) of Winnipeg, Canada, executive director of the Canadian Lutheran Council, and Dr. Carl E. Lund-Quist (right) of Geneva, Switzerland, executive secretary of the Lutheran World Federation (1954).

Above: In Russia in 1923, Herbert Hoover, then American Relief Administrator, consulted with W. L. Scheding, European commissioner of the NLC.

Below: A Russian sign indicating the council's participation in Hoover's American Relief Administration.

AMERICAN RELIEF ADMINISTRATION KITCHEN
SUPPORTED BY THE
NATIONAL LUTHERAN COUNCIL OF AMERICA

АМЕРИКАНСКАЯ АДМИНИСТРАЦИЯ ПОМОЩИ
СТОЛОВАЯ
АМЕРИКАНСКОГО НАЦИОНАЛЬНОГО ЛЮТЕРАНСКОГО
СОБОРА

Right (on opposite
Refugees along a I
road in

Above: Headquarters of the NI
at 50 Madison Avenue, New Yc
City (1950-66).

Left: Korean refugee children receive food through NLC-sponsored
agencies.

Opposite page: Top left: on
many Lutheran World Action
drive posters. Top right: the
blem of Lutheran World I
featuring "love's working arm."
low: Hong Kong women wo:
at one of the crafts sponsore
the LWF's self-help program.

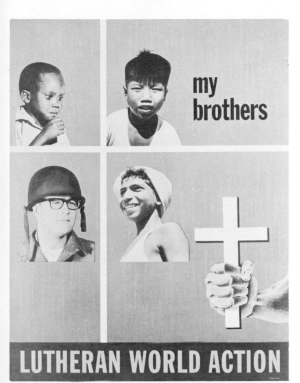

my
brothers

LUTHERAN WORLD ACTION

LWR

Above: Dr. Daniel Nelson and three Chinese friends.

Below: Dr. Nelson and a Chinese delegation on the way to an Oslo conference in 1947. They are in front of the airplane "St. Paul" flown by Dr. Nelson on hundreds of church missions.

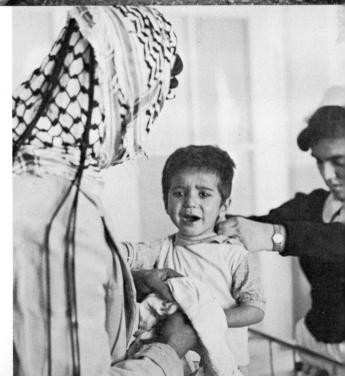

Above: Lutheran World Action funds helped support work in missions orphaned by the war, such as Tanganyika.

Right: An Arab father brings his son for treatment in the children's ward of Augusta Victoria Hospital in Jerusalem.

Above: Hong Kong residents line up for aid at the Lutheran World Service mobile clinic.

Below: Officials of Lutheran World Relief and Lutheran World Action in 1959 celebrated the fact that LWR shipments that year passed the $100 million mark.

Above: Typical scene in European refugee camp where Lutheran funds helped process these war victims for resettlement in other parts of the world.

Right: LWA funds helped reconstruct war-torn churches of Europe such as this one in Stuttgart.

Above: Students
worship in the Luth-
an Student House
the University of M
nesota, one of the
erations of the NL
Division of Coll
and University Wo

Left: The Rev. Wal
Kloetzli, secretary f
Urban Church Pla
ning in the Division
American Missions
the National Luther
Council, points out t
church potentialities
the San Francisco B
area to the Rev. R
P. Hidy, pastor of
Mark's Church there

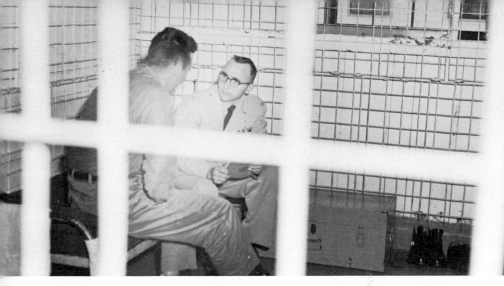

Above: A prison chaplain at work. Institutional chaplaincy was one of the areas of concern of the NLC's Division of Welfare.

Below: A chaplain conducting services for troops in Viet Nam. A religious program for the armed forces was the major concern of the NLC's Division of Service to Military Personnel.

Above: Dr. Robert E. Van Deusen (left), Washington secretary of the NLC's Division of Public Relations, met with Congressman Cleveland W. Bailey of W. Virginia in 1961 before a House Committee hearing on aid to education.

Below: Dr. Paul C. Empie, executive secretary of the NLC, demonstrated the interfaith interests of the council as he participated in the first official Lutheran-Catholic dialogue in 1965.

National Lutheran Council. The Student Commission of the Conference had been unanimously opposed to the transfer in 1942 but favored it in 1944. Schiotz noted three reasons for this changed attitude: (1) reorganization of the NLC was imminent; (2) expansion of the work was needed and staff enlargement would complicate later transfer; and (3) ULCA staff retirement made this an opportune time for change.

There were larger reasons for making student work more widely cooperative. The main one was the logic of the situation. It was clear that the church badly needed to concentrate its strength in order to get any effective foothold in the influential and secular world of higher education. It was also foreseen that the return of veterans would swell enrollments and enlarge the task. And there was the strong ferment of increasing readiness on the part of Lutherans generally to use the Council to accomplish tasks that were better done in cooperation.

To define the function of the Commission on Student Service, a fourfold statement was proposed as follows:

> to conserve the faith,
> to develop the loyalty,
> to cultivate the spiritual life of Christian students,
> to discover, develop, and direct future leaders of the church.

Added to this statement, which was directed entirely toward working with those already Christian, was a fifth phrase, namely, "to win students for Christ and His Church." [3]

Taking office as the first executive in February of 1946 was the Reverend Morris Wee.[4] In July the Commission was functioning fully, starting with a budget in excess of $100,000. By the end of the year it had five national secretaries (with headquarters in Chicago), eighteen full-time campus pastors, six part-time pastors, and fourteen full-time women counselors. It also worked with more than three hundred pastors of congregations who were designated as student pastors at no extra pay.

Especially in its earlier years, much of the Commission's work at a particular school was carried out through the local fellowship of the Lutheran Student Association of America. Organized in the 1920's, LSAA was an association of students independent of the church bodies and technically independent of the Student Commission, yet very much dependent on the latter for adult leadership and resources. Much of the counseling and teaching ministry of the campus pastors was effected through the local LSA. The Commission undertook preparation and dissemination of extensive literature for pastors and students, ranging from devotional and worship materials to study books on biblical and doctrinal themes.

Since about half the college students in 1946 were veterans, whose presence pushed up enrollments and caused housing difficulties, emergency funds were appropriated from Lutheran World Action to support ministries at particularly crowded universities and at Lutheran colleges as well.

In the 1940's student centers were found to be valuable adjuncts to denominational student work. Outlining the need for student centers in more than thirty places across the country, the Commission boldly asked the councillors for $2,310,000 for buildings from the next LWA appeal. In response the participating bodies raised $885,000 for such centers in the next half dozen years and then projected a second and third phase of this effort.

Meanwhile, immediate request for division status provoked considerable discussion. Before the Council was the suggestion that there be a division of youth work in which student work might become a department. Campus ministry people resisted this identification and favored a division of higher education, if they were not to be a separate division. A division of youth work was rejected by the Council. In the end there appeared the Division of Student Service (1949) which became in 1956 the Division of College and University Work.

College and University Work

The shift from student work to college and university work gave tone to the whole twenty years of this NLC program but was already quite discernible in the early years. The change was from the effort to preserve Lutheran students in the faith to the broad mission which the Christian faith and the church carry into the vast university world, its personnel and its thinking. By

1950 interpretations spoke of the mission to the university, and faculty seminars were major features in many campus programs. By 1952 there was the first NLC-sponsored chair of religion at a state university, the State University of Iowa. At the same time there was a more general effort—meeting with considerable success—to provide a "core curriculum" for Lutheran students and others in non-credit courses with registration fee and regular attendance required and with the campus pastor as the teacher.

This ministry to students flourished. When the Reverend Donald R. Heiges became executive secretary in 1950 there was a national staff of six (including three regional secretaries) and a local staff exceeding 400 (45 of them receiving salary from the Division). The Division prepared and distributed a dozen items of literature, conducted its own annual staff conference and helped with the LSAA's national conference. Its national staff provided extended field services. It carried through three study-work projects in Europe under Lutheran World Federation sponsorship, and helped foreign students in America in several ways, including the location of displaced persons in the student category. In 1952 Heiges could report that this ministry touched 600 of the 1,800 colleges and universities in the United States, operating under a budget approaching $200,000.

Another significant trend in the ever-changing campus ministry was directed toward a more churchly program on the campus itself. The earlier pattern had stressed the LSA program and sought to relate students to neighboring congregations for worship. After 1950 the trend was toward providing a full-orbed Christian ministry in the university setting, either through worship on campus led by the campus pastor, or through a congregation formed largely with student and faculty membership. This new development not only provided opportunity for friction with local congregations, it also brought the NLC directly into the work of supporting congregational life itself. Once again the need for particular services brought an appropriate response from Council personnel, even though the formal rules for the Council were strained in the process.

A three-paragraph interpretation of its function in an annual report of the Division provides a concise summary as follows:

"It is the function of the Division to assist congregations, foundations, directing committees, districts, conferences, and synods to meet the challenge of the campus, and to coordinate, deepen, and expand student service throughout the country. In the process of carrying out this function the Division has established certain standards for student work. This work can be approached either as a ministry to students or as a program for students.

"An effective ministry to students ought to exhibit the following emphases: *Preaching*, or proclaiming the Word; *Teaching*, or interpreting the Word in relation to all aspects of human existence; *Counseling*, or helping students solve their problems; *Calling*, or taking the initiative to seek out students where they are; *Recruiting*, or enlisting students for service to Christ and the Church.

"An effective student program ought to be characterized by the following emphases: *Worship*—attendance at the regular Sunday morning services of a local congregation and at Holy Communion, participation in informal group worship, and development of daily personal devotions; *Study*—primarily of the Bible, but also of the confessions, the history and work of the Church, and the Christian life; *Evangelism*—personal witness to Christ as well as the witness of the Christian community within the university; *Service*—training in stewardship, assistance in local congregations, support of relief and rehabilitation projects, etc.; *Recreation*—wholesome opportunities for fun, fellowship and friendship." [5]

American Missions Advances

In describing the rising tide of the Council's work in postwar years certain new programs in other areas of domestic service provide highlights.

The Division of American Missions began a Department of Rural Church Life in 1945 which has had a quiet effectiveness for twenty years in stimulating Lutheran churches to a new awareness of the needs and opportunities of rural America, and of the church's responsibility and resources for meeting those needs and opportunities. Informational bulletins and other publications, lectures and speeches have held this area of concern before the consciousness of Lutherans. Developing fruitful contacts with state and federal agricultural agencies has been another major accomplishment of the secretary in this field, together with development of statistical studies setting forth trends in Lutheran rural life. A major instrument has been the holding of conferences and institutes, increasingly geared to be helpful for a particular area or locality, thus encouraging coordinated planning and helpful liaison between rural pastors and resource people in other aspects of community life.

Within the same Division a Department for the Christian Approach to the Jewish People was established in 1947. The main purpose was twofold: "to remind our churches that the gospel is for the Jew also, and to assist the churches in bringing the gospel to the Jewish people." Its main emphasis lay in bringing into the life of Lutheran congregations conscious evangelism efforts in behalf of the Jew. It also became active in coordination and sharing among half a dozen established Lutheran missions to the Jews in major cities and initiated special work in several other metropolitan areas. Like all such efforts at evangelizing Jews, results were quite limited in terms of accessions.

Special work in Negro communities was undertaken by the Division of American Missions in 1951. Initially a cooperative program of the American Lutheran Church and the Augustana Lutheran Church, with contributions from several other bodies, a major responsibility was the supervision and cultivation of more than a dozen Negro congregations turned over to the Council by the American Lutheran Church. In 1955 that church resumed direct responsibility from the NLC in order to integrate the Negro work with other mission work. Meanwhile, the secretary in this field developed consultative services to Lutheran congregations in communities of racial transition and assisted all the church bodies in planning new mission work in Negro communities.

The Division also had a mandate and a staff member in the area of Urban Church Planning, beginning in 1951, but full development for this field belongs to the next period of Council history.

In 1946 Executive Secretary Hoyer, anticipating the end of work with wartime temporary communities and under the necessity of moving from an emergency budget to a permanent one, asked in behalf of his Division: "Quo Vadis?" As it turned out, the ministry to temporary communities continued on a reduced scale and the comity tasks with regional committees continued to have major importance. New directions in American missions were found in focusing attention on specialized situations—rural and urban—and on special, minority groups—Jews and Negroes. This kind of service, providing resources for highly specialized tasks, was a natural one for a national cooperative organization in its ongoing and routine role.

Other Program Advances

Outstanding among the program advances in the Division of Welfare during this period was the addition of a consultant in the field of institutional chaplaincies. This work, begun in 1945, quickly proved quite useful in organizing a spiritual-social ministry to hospitalized veterans. Working in close association with the chief of chaplains of the Veterans Administration of the federal government, the consultant set up a system of Lutheran contact pastors for the increasing number of veterans hospitals. In 1949 there were 136 such hospitals to which Lutheran clergymen were related, including 38 full-time Lutheran chaplains. These services were expanded to include mental and general hospitals and penal institutions. The Council's staff man made surveys, provided consultation in the field, and provided literature and other resources for chaplains and other pastors serving institutions. This NLC service was recognized as outstanding in its field.

In the Division of Public Relations a major addition was the Washington office, established to facilitate liaison with the federal government in 1948. Comparable to the office created for a short time during World War I by the National Lutheran Soldiers' and Sailors' Commission, this post was filled by a Lutheran clergyman, Robert E. Van Deusen, with increasing usefulness for eighteen years until the Council's demise. The Washington secretary has maintained effective channels of communication, informing key churchmen about contemporary events in the federal government and informing key government officials about current programs and thinking in the Lutheran church. He has conducted research on government procedures and on new legislation and reported the pertinent facts for churchmen. He represented the National Lutheran Council on various inter-church committees and at conferences in his field and kept the participating bodies informed about legislative hearings. He helped to keep before the Lutheran public the major issues of church and state. His role became an essential one for the Lutheran churches he served.

The total domestic program grew until the regular budget in 1951 exceeded half a million dollars—twenty times the budget of twenty years earlier! Such expansion bears eloquent testimony to the fact that the participating bodies found their cooperative activity increasingly useful.

The Church Abroad

By far the largest and most spectacular advance of the NLC in postwar years was its overseas activities. Actually this story should rather be viewed as a dramatic Christian-to-Christian and human-to-human outpouring of great quantities of concern and help that crossed oceans to minister to the needs of destitute, afflicted, and nearly hopeless millions in Europe and other continents as well. It has its heart-ringing cries for help and its heart-warming ministry of compassion. It has its bold heroes and its corps of dedicated, self-sacrificing servants. It is an intensely human story. Unfortunately, here there is only space to outline its features in the perspective of the Council's organizational history.[6]

At the end of 1944 the Reverend Paul C. Empie, newly appointed assistant to Dr. Long charged with the Lutheran World Action appeals, noted that the new appeal would stress "the Church Abroad" rather than the ministry to military personnel and indicated that this would make the task more difficult. Long, adding that "the needs for post-war reconstruction will be enormous," asserted that "the future of the Lutheran Church of the world depends in no small degree upon the vigor of the Lutherans in America in carrying forward a real program of rehabilitation. For that day and its responsibilities we must prepare now." [7] By giving about two and one-third million dollars in 1945 American Lutherans showed their willingness to help the church abroad and encouraged LWA planners to ask for an unprecedented ten million in the two years 1946-1947. This goal too was reached and exceeded, undergirding with marvelous resources the aid programs Lutheran leaders were launching.

In part this success was due to the appalling facts themselves which were widely known by the American public. One 1944 report by the United Nations Relief and Rehabilitation Administration (UNRRA) painted this shocking picture:

> Never before in the history of mankind have men been called upon to solve a relief problem of greater magnitude and complexity than that resulting from the present war. Within three years 35 countries, spread over Europe and Asia and containing more than a half a billion people, have passed under the Axis yoke. They have been robbed of their wealth, their economies have been destroyed, and their peoples have been left in semi-starvation.

The report indicated that there were probably 30 million displaced persons scattered over Europe and added as concrete illustration:

> There are 1,800,000 Frenchmen in Germany; to move this number of persons will take 24 trains a day, every day, for eight months.[8]

As American Lutherans were to learn, UNRRA's statistics and that organization's massive material aid entirely ignored the human misery and need within the enemy nations. And the peacemaking itself was to create another stream of refugees.

Successful LWA Appeals

Success for LWA appeals also reflected simple Christian stewardship, Lutheran loyalty, and effective cultivation by the organized appeals themselves. With efficient machinery already in operation for a number of years, the 1946-1947 campaign took on an added intensity. "We sense," the councillors declared, "that in this climactic crisis of humanity's history there comes a clear divine call to the Church of Jesus Christ to rise to her opportunity to be a witnessing Church. . . . In the achievement of this a grand demonstration of Christian love and benevolence is called for in the spirit of God's unspeakable love to all mankind." [9] A year later, in 1947, after hearing eyewitness accounts of the tragic physical and spiritual conditions abroad the councillors became still more urgent:

> Our hearts are deeply shocked and our spirits profoundly stirred. Truly catastrophic are the implications of the present situation. The life and health of our Church abroad and at home are at stake. We cannot sit by indifferently and with idle hands at a time when millions of souls and the fruit of centuries of Lutheran achievement are thus gravely jeopardized. . . . It is solemn and awful to realize that we hold in our hands the welfare and ultimate fate of so many of our Christian brethren. [10]

Basic to the campaign itself was the dissemination of volumes of information. It opened with about twenty promotional meetings throughout America to help key leaders—national, regional, and area LWA directors—plan the appeal for their congregations. Each of these 700 persons received a monthly bulletin from the NLC, and 8,500 pastors, who were key men in the actual fund-raising, received each month a different bulletin filled with information about the current situation abroad. In addition to the usual pamphlets, offering devices and bulletins, the needs were delineated in a picture brochure called "Atoning Power for the Atomic Age," which proved popular and reached a printing of more than a million copies. The News Bureau turned out many stories for the church press. Added to former audio-visual aids was a forty-minute dramatic sound motion picture titled "The Good Fight," first of a long series of Lutheran World Action films. On the local level an every-member visitation was recommended to reach all the people with the message. In addition, 447 rallies were held in which outstanding speakers helped to build enthusiasm. One of the fruits of these rallies, according to

Empie, was "the greatest nation-wide publicity in the secular press our Lutheran Church has ever had."

The response, an outpouring of $10,502,356 in two years, was gratifying. Lutherans were ready, when they heard the urgent story, to give their money generously to help their brethren abroad. This was the peak of LWA collections. Yet this appeal, annually pursued, has had surprising staying-power, in contrast to the experience in the 1920's. With considerable misgivings, councillors voted a goal of four million for 1948 which was exceeded slightly. Then gifts dropped off slowly. Officials planned to put a shrinking LWA item into regular denominational budgets. But world turmoil kept the needs at a high and highly visible level (Korean War, Hungarian revolt, new refugee waves from behind the iron curtain, etc.). After three years in which offerings were less than three million annually, the 1955 appeal exceeded that amount and each year a larger total was received. After twenty-five years (1965) an aggregate of 78 million had been raised.

Wise promotion contributed to this sustained success. Then too, Americans had for the most part rejected isolationism by this time. Starting in 1949 Lutherans joined with other Christian denominations in a simultaneous appeal called "One Great Hour of Sharing," using the fourth Sunday in Lent and taking advantage of openings given by the mass communications media. Equally important was the rising sense of worldwide fellowship among Lutherans themselves. The pattern is part of a broader maturing of American Lutheranism whereby Lutheran churches began to gain self-assurance and to take their place among other groups in the mainstream of American and international events.

Raising seventy-eight million dollars is a notable achievement for the National Lutheran Council. It eliminates any Lutheran pride, however, to note that the Jews of the United States—less numerous than Lutherans—undertook to raise more than 100 million dollars for the United Jewish Appeal in the one year of 1965 though that appeal is not strictly comparable to LWA. For the Council it has meant that LWA and the symbol of arm-and-cross have become familiar household items for millions of Americans

and that the appeal has inspired confidence and respect for the
NLC among Lutheran church officials. Above all, it has provided
the sinews for forceful intersynodical action on many fronts of
interchurch aid and service to human need.

Lutheran World Relief

An important companion to LWA was Lutheran World Relief.
Though separately incorporated and not a part of the NLC,
LWR has functioned since its beginning, in the fall of 1945, as
the material aid program of the Council, and Council staff have
been the main administrators of its program of overseas physical
relief—Ralph Long, Clarence Krumbholz, and for two decades
Bernard A. Confer. President of LWR through its first two decades has been the Reverend Franklin C. Fry, president of the
ULCA and its successor (in 1962), the Lutheran Church in America. In 1953 the Lutheran Church—Missouri Synod agreed to use
LWR facilities in its work of overseas material aid.

First organized to reach Germany and Finland with emergency
material relief because these lands were excluded from UNRRA
help, LWR soon broadened its outreach, eventually including 42
countries. By 1952 the total value of its shipments of food, clothing, and medicines exceeded $22,000,000. By 1965 this total value
had risen to $172,000,000, in the form of more than a billion
pounds of relief goods. The clothing was secured through annual
collections in Lutheran congregations and shipped to LWR ware-
houses on the east and west coasts, where it was processed and
shipped overseas. In some years the food was purchased or gathered directly from farmers (sometimes through cooperative Lutheran efforts to fill freight cars). In later years food was mainly
U.S. government surplus. Altogether government-donated com-
modities provided more than half of the value of LWR shipments.

For some of its work LWR maintained its own staff to facilitate distribution; frequently, however, it worked through the
staff of other organizations such as the Lutheran World Federation and the World Council of Churches. Its help was given on
the basis of need without regard to religious affiliation, but chan-

nels of church organizations in the receiving countries were used as much as possible in order to provide inexpensive distribution and strengthen the local church agencies. Thus LWR was a type of interchurch aid rather than simply material relief.

Lutheran World Relief joins Lutheran World Action in registering a remarkable achievement in cooperative action among America's Lutherans.

Established Relationships

The story of the National Lutheran Council's role in European relief and rehabilitation following World War II invites comparison with the similar effort after the previous war. In the 1940's the size of the operation was much greater, with two-thirds of the LWA goal of ten million dollars allotted for this work. As has been noted, American Lutherans were much better prepared the second time. They had been planning for many months. For years they had been working with refugees and orphaned missions in organized fashion. They had $200,000 set aside ahead of time.

Significantly, patterns of cooperation with non-Council Lutherans had also been set up before the war's end. An agreement with Missouri Synod Lutherans in giving aid to orphaned missions had been in effect for several years, though the Missourians were not entirely satisfied with the limitations of their role in this matter. In 1944, final arrangements were made between the American Section of the Lutheran World Convention and the Emergency Planning Council of the Missouri Synod. It was agreed that their total ministry would be offered in the name of the Lutheran World Convention and administered by a committee of five, of whom two would be Missourians. When the first commission went to Europe in 1945, one of the three was a Missouri Lutheran. This kind of cooperation continued throughout postwar years.

The Missouri Synod was related to the NLC in the 1940's in a manner roughly similar to that of the Iowa Synod in the Council's earliest days. That is to say, each was careful to maintain its distance from the Council and to limit its cooperation to externals and clearly specified tasks. On the other hand, each was greatly concerned about an effective overseas ministry and anxious to coordinate American Lutheran efforts in serving their European brethren in need. This is an indication of the progress in inter-Lutheran relations, since Missouri had been entirely separate in this work in the earlier period, and the Iowa Synod (in the American Lutheran Church) was now thoroughly a part of the Council itself.

Then, too, it is important to note that Lutherans in the 1940's knew how to relate to each other across synodical lines much better than they had in the 1920's. In the earlier period there had been much more misunderstanding and ill will. The Iowa Synod was for a time half in and half out of the Council. Some of its spokesmen (and some Missourians as well) were publicly and harshly critical of Council policies. In the 1940's relationships were more carefully worked out and criticisms were dissolved or muted. Lutherans were learning how to work together. One major reason for this was that the NLC had been working at this very role for nearly three decades and knew how to go about it.

Another reason for better inter-Lutheran relations in America in the 1940's and another evidence of the difference made by preparation and previous experience was the role of the Lutheran World Convention. Though virtually defunct in Europe during the war, the LWC was kept alive by the American Section which functioned as the Executive Committee during war years. And the American Section worked quite closely with the NLC, Ralph Long being central to both structures. When the war was ending Americans did not need to start from scratch and create ties with Europeans but could reestablish LWC ties more readily and speedily. Similarly, it was less difficult to bring European Lutherans together, even though Nazi conquests had made Germans very unpopular, so that world Lutheranism could assemble in Sweden as early as 1947.

On the other hand, neither the relief work nor the reestablishment of a world Lutheran organization was an easy task. There were formidable obstacles; once again courageous and pioneer churchmanship was called forth in behalf of large Lutheran cooperative undertakings.

Overseas Contacts

In February 1945, before the fighting in Europe had ended, three Americans—Long, Lawrence Meyer of the Missouri Synod, and P. O. Bersell, President of the Augustana Synod—traveled to Sweden and to Geneva. Though the Swedish Lutherans were not enthusiastic about renewed organizational ties with the Germans, a liaison committee for LWC was set up. It soon became a relief committee, with Fry and Long as the American members. In Geneva arrangements were made to coordinate Lutheran relief and reconstruction with that of the World Council of Churches, which was a going concern though only provisionally organized until its first assembly in 1948. Here too advanced preparation made speedy action possible.

Long returned to Europe late in 1945 and repeatedly in the next two years. His energies and wise leadership were directed almost entirely to the overseas program. In 1946 he found that 75% of his correspondence was in behalf of the Lutheran World Convention (or, rather, its intended successor, the Lutheran World Federation). Concerning 1947 he could report that "the major portion" of his time was similarly spent, so that there was "little time left to devote to the domestic program." The new constitution with its divisional committees and divisional executives proved providential in enabling Long to concentrate in one field without losing momentum for the NLC in other areas.

Thus Sylvester C. Michelfelder had considerable support at home and many contacts abroad when he set out for Europe in July of 1945 as a latter-day Morehead, commissioned to represent American Lutherans in offering physical and spiritual assistance. Michelfelder, an ALC pastor on leave from his Toledo congregation, had had years of experience with the NLC and was Long's close friend. It is the judgment of all who knew him and his work in Europe that he was providentially chosen for this task as emissary. His ability to improvise and to get by all obstacles was invaluable in this role and quite reminiscent of Morehead's earlier accomplishments. His easy friendliness, his warmth of personality, and his depth of commitment to the nurture of human life and the church in Europe epitomized for many Europeans the best that American Christians represented. He stayed in his new and strenuous tasks until his tragic death in 1951.

Michelfelder's story belongs to the Lutheran World Federation and the World Council of Churches more than it belongs to the National Lutheran Council.[11] Starting out as representative of the American Section of the Lutheran World Convention, he became in a few months the acting executive secretary for the Lutheran World Federation, both while it was being formed and during its first four years. His office in Geneva was at the gate house for the buildings which housed the budding World Council of Churches, and he was expected to work through the newly formed Department of Reconstruction and Interchurch Aid. When it quickly became clear that material relief, food and clothing to save lives, would be major church tasks, especially within the defeated nations, Michelfelder was asked by the World Council of Churches, in November of 1945, to organize a Division of Material Aid as part of the Department of Reconstruction and Interchurch Aid. He shouldered all these tasks willingly and resigned his Toledo congregation.

By October Michelfelder had helped to get the international relief agencies in Geneva to issue a strongly-worded appeal to alert public opinion to the desperate needs in Europe and to get officials of the victorious nations to take more adequate steps in providing relief. Especially frustrating was the inability of American Lutherans to get supplies into Germany. Michelfelder urged Long to appeal to government officials in the United States to modify their "hard line" policy enough to allow private agencies to send in relief supplies. In America the Council took up the cause, joining with many other forces that were objecting to American occupation policy. The councillors at their January meeting mentioned Japan, China, and Hungary, as well as Germany, and affirmed:

> We express it as our firm conviction that one means of securing a just and durable peace is to permit Christian forces of our nation to minister to human needs, wherever existent, whether those of Ally or former enemy.[12]

By March of 1946 government policy changed so that relief operations in Germany could become a major operation for Lutherans and for other agencies.

Meanwhile Michelfelder had set up an organization for the flow of foodstuffs and clothing into his Geneva warehouse and out to meet needs anywhere in Europe as they were reported to him from his correspondents in the capitals of many nations.

One of his letters, written in April of 1946, gives the flavor of his labors and something of his own zest in the work: [13]

> I am buying $5000 worth of wheat and flax seed for Hungary, for sowing immediately. I hope to find it in Switzerland. I have had a telephone offer of 500 tons of sugar—think of it!—in a country which is short of sugar. I have also had an offer of 50 tons of honey from South America. . . . I am preparing a cargo of stuff—including material aid and textbooks—for Roumania, together with a truck, which will be shipped by sea from Marseilles to Constanza. Dr. Cockburn just handed me a letter from the "Institute of Orthodox Theology" in Paris, asking for the purchase of about one thousand dollars worth of furniture, including beds, chairs, and tables. So, you see, we get theology and furniture all mixed up in the same letter.

From time to time Michelfelder was joined in this work by other American Lutheran representatives, who mainly functioned as field agents visiting certain countries to maintain liaison, to assess the needs, and to facilitate the distribution of money or material supplies. Sometimes as many as a half-dozen men would be stationed in Europe representing the American Section of the Lutheran World Federation or Lutheran World Relief. As we shall see, the refugee work brought an even larger American staff into Europe. In relief and reconstruction work an effort was made to keep outside staff and organization to a minimum.

Church Reconstruction

Church reconstruction was to become the largest part of this work. It got underway a little more slowly than relief work, but it was never lost to the sight of the American representatives because it was the distinctive task for which church people in America were prepared to give help. Norway and Finland were each given a million dollars for this purpose. In Finland 40 per cent of the total was allocated to the rebuilding of churches and parsonages, 30 per cent was designated for schools and deaconess institutions, and the remainder was used for a variety of scholarships, emergency assistance to pastors, a fund for the work of the Lutheran World Federation in Finland, etc. Through wise investment the million dollars was used for several times its value in Finland.

Germany received the largest share of the money for church reconstruction. There were gifts for ecclesiastical robes and deaconess garbs, for paper for the printing of religious matèrials, for office supplies, and for welfare institutions. Between 1947 and 1949 thirty-one "rubble churches" were erected with the help of American gifts, so named because they used salvaged brick and were inexpensively built. After 1948 help for building was mostly in the form of loans with liberal terms for repayment. American gifts, of course, could only help with a small part of the total task of rebuilding German churches. There were also gifts for rest opportunities for overburdened pastors, for theological conferences and Christian education, for new evangelism efforts such as the Evangelical Academies, etc. Meanwhile, the German churches were not only helping with material relief programs in their own land, but by 1951 West German churches were listed as "giving churches" instead of receiving ones, though the situation in East Germany under Communist rule remained bleak.

These few paragraphs describing the relief and reconstruction efforts of America's Lutherans following World War II arc but a shorthand summary of a vast volume of service to countless individuals, congregations, and national churches. Nor can one catch in a few phrases the spiritual significance of these deeds which Michelfelder termed "the Gospel of the Inasmuch." The records are filled with expressions of gratitude which indicate in small measure what these gifts have meant in strengthening the faith and the hold on life of numerous recipients and what they have meant in raising the morale of European Lutheran leaders. Clearly Americans in return learned something new about stewardship and sharing, not to mention lessons in the power of cooperative endeavor.

A Lutheran World Federation

Only a little less obvious were the gains in brotherhood and mutual association among Lutherans of various parts of the world. While Americans provided the initiative and the major resource, Lutheran churches of other lands pitched in as they were able, the Swedish church being the earliest and most obvious example. As at Eisenach in 1923, the World Assembly at Lund in 1947 built upon a large platform of good will sustained by the vast volume of interchurch aid.

Ralph Long and several of the councillors and leaders of the National Lutheran Council put much thought and effort into reconstituting a world Lutheran organization. In the summer of 1946 in Sweden they were able to bring together an international executive committee with Archbishop Eidem of Sweden as the president. On the following June 174 official representatives of Lutheran churches from 23 nations assembled at Lund in Sweden to constitute the First Assembly of the Lutheran World Federation. Forty-four American delegates and 55 German church leaders were present. A constitution was adopted providing for a continuing staff, thus making the organization a real federation, in contrast to the older title which implied only the occasional assembly or convention. It was this form, a federation, which John A. Morehead had suggested as early as 1919.

Archbishop Eidem became president and Michelfelder the executive secretary. Central offices were retained at the World Council headquarters in Geneva. By this act and by one of its stated purposes—"To foster Lutheran participation in ecumenical movements"—the new Federation announced a positive and cooperative attitude toward other churches and interdenominational cooperation, though some American participants remained ambivalent toward the ecumenical movement.

In keeping with the provisions of the new Federation a National Committee for the Lutheran World Federation in the United States took the place of the former American Section of the Lutheran World Convention. By agreement in the United States the executive committee of the National Lutheran Council became this national committee for the Federation. As Long pointed out, the NLC thereby assumed larger responsibilities and increasing importance. This arrangement was also more efficient.

Ralph Long and Paul Empie

Another transition for the Council was occasioned by the untimely death of Ralph Long in February of 1948. For eighteen years he had been the guiding spirit of the NLC. They were crucial years. His quiet forcefulness, his vision of the Council's role, and his statesmanlike planning and counsel had given him a leadership among Lutherans which had greatly enhanced the organization he served. During his earliest days in office his vigorous commitment was a major factor in the Council's continuation. During war and postwar years his energy and talents were equal to the emergencies in planning wisely for the Council's spurting growth. He joined Lauritz Larsen and John A. Morehead as men who burned themselves out in rich service at the helm of the National Lutheran Council.

Throughout its history the National Lutheran Council has been blessed in its top leadership. Long's assistant for several years was ready and qualified to step into his shoes. He quickly won the confidence of councillors, staff, and leaders of American and world Lutheranism, so that there was no faltering in the Council's ongoing effectiveness. Paul C. Empie, ULCA pastor from eastern Pennsylvania, had participated in directing LWA appeals as a young pastor in the early 1940's. As the full-time assistant to Long, starting in 1944, he had done outstanding work in directing the appeals. This continued to be true to the end of the Council's days. Still youthful in 1948, Empie continued the Long tradition with vigor and ability. In eighteen years as its Executive Director, Empie put his own mark upon the Council's achievements. Noted for his integrity and his intense desire to serve human need in the light of the Gospel, Paul Empie helped to make the Council outstanding as a steady and reliable instrument for the Lutherans of America in their thrust to identify with the perplexing worldwide problems of modern society and their passion to serve the world's needy. It is indicative of Empie's emphasis, and in keeping with the tasks he inherited from Long, that he chose to con-

tinue in the overseas arm of the Council's work when the NLC
ended and its tasks were divided.

Refugees

The years 1948-1952 were transitional in other ways as well.
Domestic programs, which had been responses to emergency and
financed by LWA funds, were settled into more permanent
status and worked into the regular budget. A desk on European
Affairs was established and manned in order to facilitate the flow
of accurate and up-to-date information from the European operations of the Council. In reporting on the transitions of 1948 Empie
concluded that the Council "gave evidence to the Church that
it is adjusting intelligently to a pattern of service carefully integrated to function smoothly with other boards and agencies of
the participating bodies."

Two facets of the Council's overseas role, in the period between
the Lund and the Hannover (1952) Assemblies, remain to be described briefly: a new phase of refugee work and a new phase
for orphaned missions responsibilities.

The whole twentieth century has been termed the century of
the refugee. In 1948 there were three categories of them in Europe: about three quarters of a million Displaced Persons, those
who could not return to their homelands for the most part because of Communist regimes; 13 million ethnic Germans ex-
pelled from neighboring countries into Germany; and an increasing stream of those flowing from iron curtain countries. Even
before Lund the LWF had set up a unique program of spiritual
ministry to the Lutheran DP's in Germany, about 150,000 Baltic
Lutherans. Young American volunteers—many years before the
Peace Corps—joined paid workers in an imaginative ministry in
and beyond the DP camps. It was felt that personal envoys who
could concretely embody American concern for refugees were an
important accompaniment of the gifts themselves. Under the direction of Howard Hong, St. Olaf College professor sent to Europe by the USA Committee of the LWF, the program included
provision of religious literature, supporting and equipping DP
pastors in their itinerant ministry from camp to camp, and the

operation of two leadership training schools with short-term courses and fellowship opportunities for Christian workers among the refugees themselves.

After the Lund Assembly the Lutheran World Federation set up a Resettlement Division with Stewart W. Herman, ULCA clergyman, as its first executive. At the same time (summer of 1948) the United States Congress passed a law admitting a number of DP's for settlement under careful conditions. LWF opened a network of twenty-four offices in western Germany to process DP's. A year later it was also able to prepare ethnic Germans for resettlement. From Geneva contacts were established with receiving countries all over the world. While not an NLC program, this European machinery was largely staffed by Americans and financed by LWA.

Work with refugees, of course, straddled the oceans and represented a sizeable domestic program in the United States. Under the aegis of Clarence F. Krumbholz and the Division of Welfare, a Lutheran Resettlement Service was established in October of 1948 within the NLC. Its functions were: to secure assurances for jobs and housing for DP's; to serve as the contact office between sponsors in America and the LWF staff in Europe in the processing and selecting of DP's; to receive and send to their destination the refugees on their arrival in the United States; and to offer consultation and service in the adjustment of DP's in the United States. State and area committees were organized to carry out local responsibilities. There was a special program for orphaned DP children and a program, in charge of the Division of American Missions, to help DP pastors settle in America and develop a useful ministry, usually to the larger concentrations of their own people. At its peak the staff included 125 people.

By 1952 the program was greatly reduced and awaited further government action, except for continuing services in helping refugees adjust. Since 1948 36,000 Europeans had been resettled in the United States, each individual or family having had its own particular destination assured ahead of time in order to comply with the law. Several thousand of these were ethnic Germans rather than DP's. Expenditures for this program exceeded

$3,000,000, but much of it was returned as repayment for loans. In charge of this work was Miss Cordelia Cox.

The values experienced in this cooperative undertaking were incalculable, not only in a new start for thousands of people, but also in enrichment of many American communities and many Lutheran congregations. Here was another instance, perhaps the mostly vividly personal one, in which an NLC program entered directly into the life of a great number of congregations of the participating bodies.

CYCOM

After World War II the Council's responsibility for orphaned missions increased rather than decreased. From 1939 through 1947 the NLC channeled two and one-half million dollars into this work. From 1948 to 1952 the amount was three and a half million dollars. In 1949 sixteen of the fields assisted were formerly those of German societies, while two had been Finnish and three were autonomous younger churches. Geographic representation included East Africa, South Africa, Southwest Africa, Borneo, China, India, Indonesia, Japan, New Guinea, and Palestine. German missionaries could not return after the war and European societies lacked resources to provide more than token help. Meanwhile the needs and opportunities increased. Most of the money was used to support missionaries but some was used for Bibles and other printed materials, or, occasionally, to help with food and clothing.

Recognizing the continuing nature of its responsibility, the NLC in 1948 organized a Commission on Younger Churches and Orphaned Missions (CYCOM). Able administration was given by Reverend Fredrik A. Schiotz. In scope of activity and in budget CYCOM exceeded the work of the International Missionary Council with other Protestant orphaned missions. The tasks were mainly the administration of funds and coordination of services. Council staff on the fields numbered about a half a dozen. These men did pioneering work, often under trying circumstances. By ingenuity and persistence, for example, the Reverend Edwin Moll was able to salvage very valuable properties for the LWF which had been taken over by the Jordanian government in Palestine and to secure one million dollars indemnity from the Israeli government. And the Reverend Daniel Nelson had become almost legendary in China before his martyr's death in 1948. He had put to use an airplane, renamed the St. Paul, which did yeoman service in transporting missionaries and supplies and finally underwent thrilling adventures in rescuing missionaries from the conquering Communists in China.

Large properties of Lutheran mission fields in Tanganyika were transferred to the National Lutheran Council, beginning in 1949, as the only way of keeping them in Lutheran hands. The work on the mainland of China was closed out in 1951 with the Communist take-over. In that same year Schiotz was able to report that field cooperation, that had been forced on Lutheran groups during war emergencies, had now become accepted practice with the formation of constitutions for five Lutheran Mission Councils on five of the fields.

Meanwhile CYCOM was midwife for the birth of the Department of World Missions of the LWF. CYCOM carried the administration for annual meetings of a Commission on World Missions and prepared the proposal that a department (with staff and continuing responsibilities) be organized. At the Hannover Assembly in 1952 this step was taken and thereafter all the work with orphaned missions was transferred to the international organization, except the Tanganyika fields for which the NLC continued to take responsibility.

Through CYCOM the National Lutheran Council, in behalf of America's Lutherans, was able to lead in weaving a network of mutually valuable associations that bound together in Christian service the people of many nations on many continents, helping Lutheranism to be truly worldwide.

Between the first assembly of the Lutheran World Federation at Lund in 1947 and the second assembly at Hannover, Germany, in 1952 the LWF had entered into many programs, mostly connected with interchurch aid and mostly supported by LWA funds. At Hannover the organization was stabilized and put on a regular rather than an emergency basis. The Reverend Carl Lund-Quist, who had been Empie's assistant director in the National Lutheran Council and then for more than a year Michelfelder's assistant in Geneva, succeeded Michelfelder as executive secretary of the LWF. With the establishment of a Department of World Service and a Department of World Missions for LWF the National Lutheran Council relinquished its predominating role. Thereafter it functioned as an important national segment of an international Lutheranism.

Fine Middle-Aged Fettle

Thus 1952 marks the end of the postwar crescendo in the Council's history. Some emergencies had passed; other emergency situations became temporary or permanent aspects of a "normal" or routine Council program. Even the annual LWA appeal became accepted and ongoing procedure. The formation of the Canadian Lutheran Council, as well as the LWF, defined the NLC more precisely as belonging to the United States. By 1952 it was clear that there would be no larger federation among American Lutherans in the years immediately ahead, no increase in the Council's constituency nor formation of one church from its participating bodies, since more limited mergers were the order of the day.

In a more subtle way the whole period (1946-1952) was a time of settling down, even as programs multiplied and the organization grew in unprecedented fashion. There was less of the zest and enthusiasm associated with the pioneer efforts of a new movement. There was less freedom for the executive director to be innovative and to lead in new directions. Doing things a second time produced greater efficiency but less excitement. Success and large-scale activities resulted in maturity and a complex organization, they also led to a settling down into established channels. Morale remained high. Staff people generally worked with a strong sense of mission and of teamwork. But second-generation leaders—both in the council staff and in the denominations that had been created in previous decades—slipped into routines more easily than the first generation had. The reorganization in 1945 was the sign that this change had begun and at the same time the main instrument for effecting the change. Ralph Long spanned the generations, though he did not easily fit into the more bureaucratic patterns of the later years.

In the postwar years, then, the Council waxed strong, carried through a vast volume of cooperative activities for American and world Lutheranism, and came through the emergencies in fine if somewhat middle-aged fettle.

VIII

Broad Streams of Steady Traffic (1953-1966)

In its last fourteen years the Council maintained the program patterns evolved in the postwar years with only a few exceptions. There was fairly steady growth. But there were not many breakthroughs into new areas until a change in context brought some new patterns at the same time that it brought plans to supersede the Council with new organizations. This chapter will describe the latter-day NLC in its regular work. The next one will describe the altered situation in the 1960's as the baton was handed on to a new runner for another phase of the race.

Latin America

As early as the 1930's there had been the suggestion that Lutherans in North America use the National Lutheran Council for a cooperative outreach to South America. In 1951 the Council finally set up a Division of Lutheran Cooperation in Latin America in time to help the LWF create in 1952 its Committee on Latin America. These two committees had the same executive secretary, Stewart Herman, with headquarters in New York. The NLC division committee by special agreement also served as the administrative committee for the international office, as the LWF Committee met only every 18 months. Thus the two organizations were really functioning as one. On the one hand, this arrangement enabled the spiritual ministry to Lutheran diaspora groups in Latin America to be sponsored by the LWF with money which came mainly from American sources. On the other hand, the NLC Division was authorized to develop a Spanish language mission in Uruguay. By 1953 there were nine pastors serving as staff in the field and the budget exceeded $160,000.

The NLC's work in Montevideo—subsequently in Rivera also—consisted of building normal mission congregations, in the hope that all NLC bodies would share in the common venture. Supported for four years by the Augustana Lutheran Church and the ULCA, it was then taken over from the NLC in 1956 by the Augustana Church.

Under LWF auspices a congregation was organized in Caracas, Venezuela, in 1952 with three pastors to minister in three different languages—German, Hungarian, and Latvian—and with three different "chapters" or groupings under one constitution. Later a Scandinavian chapter was formed. Services were held in as many as six languages. Elsewhere in Venezuela an itinerant ministry was established to meet the needs of European refugees and immigrants, leading eventually to the organization of three other parishes. In Colombia by a similar process five congregations were established. Work quickly got underway in Ecuador, Peru, and Mexico. Subsidies were also provided to assist established churches in Argentina, Bolivia, Brazil, and Chile, especially for the spiritual care of displaced persons. This diaspora ministry under the LWF expanded to include seventeen pastors in 1956. By the end of 1957 nearly half a million dollars—largely LWA funds—had been invested in land or buildings to support the work, usually on a revolving loan basis.

Another important task for the LWF was that of drawing the various scattered segments of Lutheranism in Latin America into an awareness of each other for mutual support and into an awareness of world Lutheranism. A number of exchange visits both within and beyond Latin America were arranged. Every three to five years an All Latin America Lutheran Conference was held. Grants to theological education, especially in the development of the Spanish-language seminary in Buenos Aires, Argentina, were intended to help provide a ministry for the whole of Latin America. Secretary Herman traveled the area extensively as the representative of the Lutheran World Federation. By 1960 this aspect of the Latin America work, inspired by the slogan "contact, consultation, cooperation," was receiving more emphasis than the diaspora ministry.

The NLC Department (changed from a Division in 1956) fostered hemispheric exchanges of personnel and recruited North American pastors for service in South America. An increasingly significant aspect of the program was the promotion and distribution of Spanish-language publications and audio-visual aids. Work was begun, for example, on a translation of Luther's writings, on a theological periodical, on a set of biblical slides, and on a New Testament commentary. In 1960 the relevant mission board of each of the participating bodies of the NLC, together with the Missouri Synod's Board of Missions, established "Publicaciones El Escudo" as an incorporated name under which to publish Lutheran literature in the Spanish language. The most important publication has been a new service book and hymnal, *Culto Christiano*.

In 1965 the LWF office for Latin America was transferred to Geneva. The NLC continued to support the international program and to maintain its own department for both direct and indirect cooperation in the Latin American work.

The Department of Lutheran Cooperation in Latin America during a dozen crucial years took basic steps to encourage in that large and potent area of the globe a Lutheranism that would grow and provide mutual support across national and linguistic boundaries, even as it found sustenance from Lutherans in Europe and North America. Beginnings were also made for an indigenous, Spanish-speaking Lutheranism.

Division of LWF Affairs

Meanwhile, in 1956, the Council had reorganized the structure for all its overseas work. A Division of Lutheran World Federation Affairs had been created with the executive committee of the Council serving as the division committee and with Stewart Herman administering the Division as well as his Department on Latin America within the Division. There were three other departments in the Division. The Department of World Missions Cooperation continued that work from CYCOM which had not been transferred to LWF, namely, the administration of three former German mission fields in Tanganyika. In the last decade of the Council this Department's budget doubled to about a million dollars annually. The Department of Lutheran World Service continued the channeling of Lutheran World Action funds into the LWF programs of interchurch aid, relief, and refugee services, spending about $875,000 in 1956 alone.

The third department, the Department on Theological Cooperation, was a new development in which the NLC followed the LWF instead of pioneering. After the Hannover Assembly of the LWF in 1952 a Committee on Theological Cooperation was formed in the United States to cooperate with the LWF Department of Theology. This Committee, and the Department when it was created, administered the American part of the exchange and scholarship program which brought European theological students to this country and sent their American counterparts to Europe. It also provided various theological conferences in America, using European lecturers, and gathered into a conference annually the foreign Lutheran theological students studying in America. The new Department served as the American agent for the LWF in theological matters in various other ways, for example, in promoting the *Lutheran World*, quarterly theological journal of the LWF.

After the Minneapolis Assembly of the Lutheran World Federation in 1957—which, incidentally, involved a major planning effort for nearly all parts of the NLC, it became obvious that a vigorous exchange program would become increasingly important for the vitality of the LWF. Staff was secured for this work, which was variously called an office or a program since its role was interrelated with the other departments, and it had considerable growth in a decade. Its impact belongs to the story told in the next chapter.

Urban Church Planning

One major development within the Division of American Missions in its last fourteen years was the office for urban church planning. Begun at about the same time as federal programs for urban renewal (1950), this type of service proved unusually pioneering and useful for Lutherans and for other denominations as well. One sentence in a 1955 report sums it up by stating that the secretary for urban church planning "has marshalled the facts, aroused the Church, outlined the techniques, and is pointing the way, both with respect to over-all need, as well as specific area or parish analysis and adjustment." [1]

The approach of this office, like much of the work of the NLC, consisted of digging out the facts with care, disseminating these facts about urban trends and church planning, and getting others on the local scene to follow suit for their own situation. Under the able leadership of the Reverend Walter Kloetzli Jr., a careful instrument was developed for the urban congregation's self-study, and methods were devised to involve a number of Lutheran congregations in a geographic area to undertake such self-study together over a specified period of months. The demand for this kind of service increased rapidly so that a second staff person was added, steps were taken to train local leadership to carry through these studies, and a half dozen or more qualified, trained study consultants were used from time to time in guiding these programs. By 1960 more than sixty area studies had been undertaken, involving over nine hundred congregations.

A logical next step was the development of strategy study and planning that would involve a whole metropolitan area and that would, hopefully, suggest to the Lutheran leaders and congregations of a city directions for the future of a coordinated Lutheranism in that whole area. In the 1960's major metropolitan studies developed in three phases: (1) an overview of the metropolitan area, including the history of its churches; (2) the congregational self-study process; and (3) strategy planning sessions involving Lutheran congregations in community groupings. From this process there evolved in Baltimore, for example, a program working toward a coordinated Lutheran witness in various areas of that city, employing a staff person who had consultative relation to the NLC.

A number of educational channels have been found to alert the church to trends in the cities and to give training to churchmen immersed in ministry within cities. There have been a number of seminars on urban problems, some of them at seminaries. Lectures and articles have told the story. Books have been published describing Lutheran urban congregations or the self-study process. Other denominations have used NLC study instruments, and the Council's staff have been leaders in ecumenical efforts to help develop a relevant ministry in the cities.

Urban church planning represents a field in which the coordinated approach through the NLC has enabled Lutherans to provide pioneer leadership during the latter days of the Council.

Other American Missions Work

In other areas of its work the Division of American Missions continued to provide the kinds of services described in previous chapters with appropriate growth and with adaptations to meet changing circumstances. In 1960 the Reverend Robert W. Long, son of Ralph Long of earlier NLC fame, became executive secretary of the Division for its last six years.

With the participating bodies founding more than a hundred new congregations each year, the twenty-six regional planning committees continued to perform a crucial coordinating function. Their tasks were defined as threefold: (1) studying mission opportunities and responsibilities in their regions; (2) ascertaining or assigning areas in which the participating bodies might carry on mission work; and (3) investigating situations of allegedly harmful duplication of work by congregations. In 1963 the committees were reduced in number to eight. At the same time study meetings were instituted in each region with general executives and missions administrators of non-Council Lutheran bodies. A comprehensive mapping project was also undertaken to show better than heretofore the location and relationships of all Lutheran congregations.

The rural or town-and-country program developed increasing

effectiveness during this period in serving the thousands of Lutheran congregations in non-metropolitan communities. The task of these congregations was "to export apostles, to serve people involved in the world's most successful agricultural enterprise, to minister to the growing number of the rural non-farm population, to strengthen their position through mergers, to assist in community development, and to relate their ministry to all of society." For such specialized tasks the secretary for town and country of the NLC, the Reverend E. W. Mueller, provided help in a number of ways, mostly educational, consultative, and coordinating. He ably represented Lutherans and a Christian point of view in a number of national organizations and conferences dealing with rural life, and, on the other hand, sought to stimulate a more positive attitude on the part of the total church to the town and country ministry. Most of his work was aimed at direct help for rural pastors and congregations. The NLC sponsored many workshops and conferences and its staff participated in many more under other auspices. Pamphlets, books, a Rural Life Sunday packet, a God-Home-Country youth program, etc., were tools found useful in this unspectacular but valuable service of cooperative Lutheranism.

A ministry to temporary communities, which loomed large for the Division of American Missions in the 1940's, continued on a smaller scale in the 1950's and 1960's, changing with the changing panorama of needs. In 1957 there were only three places where special help was supplied. In 1959 the program started to expand again to reach into emerging communities of predominantly military personnel where the turnover was too rapid for the development of a settled ministry.

The Division's responsibility to cultivate Lutheran concern for special groups has remained steady, though particular programs have changed. Work with the Jews proceeded on an even keel until it was closed out in 1962; at that time it was felt that such work should become an integral part of the evangelism tasks of the church bodies. Specific work with Negroes was lodged in a more general office of intercultural outreach in 1955 (renamed human relations in 1961), including concern for such ethnic groups as the American Indian, the Mexican, the Puerto Rican, the Oriental, and others. This office, according to one report, was "an acknowledgment that the church is aware of its mission to all conditions of men, and that it has not manifested this concern as it ought in its typical congregational life." [2] The staff secretary assembled and made available to the churches information pertaining to the cultural and religious background of these groups. He also pointed to the barriers within the church and within the groups themselves which hindered an effective outreach to them. Conferences and consultations for small groups or a local congregation helped to establish methods for a truly dynamic and inclusive outreach. Specially trained parish workers assisted congregations to face a particular challenge. In 1960, for example, field workers assisted congregations to reach out to migrant workers in Wisconsin, to the Puerto Ricans and Negroes in the Bronx, and to the Negroes, Puerto Ricans, and mountain whites in the inner city of Chicago.

Intercultural outreach, though not a major Council program, represented an important cooperative effort to tackle a serious limitation of American Lutheranism, its narrow identification with a north European background.

Radio and Television

Since 1930, when Ralph Long joined the Council, there had been a continuing interest in cooperative Lutheran programs in radio, audio-visuals, movies, and, in due time, television. Over the years a sizeable service was rendered in coordinating Lutheran participation in other programs, for example, the choice of Lutheran speakers for the "Church of the Air" radio broadcasts. But the Council's own program in this field was quite slow to develop, despite many study sessions by committees and the frequently expressed conviction that this was a promising area for cooperative Lutheran effort. For more than a year during early days of World War II NLC-sponsored broadcasts from short-wave station WRUL in Boston beamed Lutheran sermons overseas in various European languages, until the government took over the use of that station. From 1942 until 1948 the Council sponsored a "March of Faith" program over radio station

WCAL at St. Olaf College, Northfield, Minnesota. This program was also promoted as transcriptions for other radio stations.

Not until 1956, however, did the Council have a functioning Department of Radio and Television as part of its Division of Public Relations. In 1959 this Department took over responsibility for two programs which had been created by the Evangelical Lutheran Church. One of these was a 15-minute radio program called "Children's Chapel," which consisted of songs sung by a children's choir with professionally dramatized stories from the Bible. In the 1960's this program achieved a station list of 400. The second of these, "Invitation for Tomorrow," was a one-minute spot announcement for television, inviting the viewer to attend church. It was used by more than half the television stations in the United States.

Most significant of the Department's programs was "Light Time," a filmed TV series of 104 quarter-hour programs for eight-to-twelve-year-old children, aimed primarily at the unchurched and used by some 140 television stations. This program proved quite popular and received high praise for its creative presentation of the Christian message.

The Department of Radio and Television came to an end in 1964, mainly because mergers among NLC bodies brought into one church (The American Lutheran Church) most of the support for this work. More than a million dollars had been invested in its work by the five bodies which had supported it.

The production of moving pictures and other audio-visuals never became an explicit responsibility of the Council in behalf of its participating bodies. LWA produced a number of films for its own promotional purposes, as did other units of the Council occasionally. The Division of Public Relations promoted and distributed "Harvest of Years," a film depicting dramatically the history of the Lutheran church in America.

Movie-Making

But the major venture into movie-making in behalf of American Lutherans was made by forming a separate corporation.

Lutheran Church Productions, Inc., came into being in 1951 as a corporate agency of the American Lutheran Church, the Augustana Synod, the Evangelical Lutheran Church, the Lutheran Church–Missouri Synod, the United Lutheran Church in America, and the National Lutheran Council. Action was initiated by the NLC, but a separate organization was effected in order to include the Missourians as full partners. This turned out to be an important step, because, as Paul Empie judged it, "the Martin Luther film and the Lutheran Service Commission were the two joint enterprises which helped Missouri get working with the NLC the best." [3]

Lutheran Church Productions' first film, "Martin Luther," was released in 1953. It was a dramatic and effective portrayal of the Reformer's experience and was the first successful church-commissioned motion picture to be a box-office success. It not only achieved wide commercial showing and a number of awards, but has also continued to be useful beyond the demise of the National Lutheran Council itself.

In 1957 a parallel corporation was formed, Lutheran Film Associates. It prepared and presented another film, "Question 7," which dealt provocatively with the church-state struggle in East Germany. It also won high critical acclaim but less success in theater showings. In 1966 a third film, a documentary on the subject of the church and racial tensions, "A Time for Burning," was released by Lutheran Film Associates and received widespread and enthusiastic response from viewers and critics. These film organizations became a part of LCUSA in 1967.

The film endeavors, combining NLC constituency and the Missouri Synod, brought a dramatic focus upon their common heritage, and, in Empie's words, "may have done more to cement ties between Lutherans in this country than decades of theological conversations." [4]

Public Relations

When a Division of Public Relations of the NLC was created in 1945, much of the Council's domestic program of the preceding two decades fell naturally under its aegis. A Department of Public Information continued the tasks of the News Bureau and continued to carry that name. In 1949, to take a typical example, the News Bureau issued 138 releases consisting of 38 feature articles and 471 news stories plus 89 pictures. The outlets for this service were: 63 Lutheran periodicals, 57 foreign publications, 31 non-Lutheran Protestant journals, 54 religious editors for daily newspapers, four news magazines, three wire services, 58 publicity centers. In 1965 it was reported that releases were going to nearly 800 outlets, including about 200 daily newspapers, 70 radio stations, 65 Lutheran and 25 non-Lutheran publications, and about 80 foreign outlets. By that time there were three staff men in this work, including a writer stationed in Washington. They continued to participate in publicity workshops and to provide news coverage for church conventions of all kinds. Erik Modean, who for nearly twenty years headed the News Bureau, served as director of the Reporting Service for the Evanston Assembly of the World Council of Churches in 1954. Under his leadership the Bureau achieved a reputation for high professional competence.

A Department of Research and Statistics was the second department under the Division of Public Relations in the 1940's. It continued the work previously done by George Linn Kieffer, expanding in later years to include two staff persons. In the 1940's this Department produced a statistical handbook for the use of Lutheran groups. During the latter years of the Council the Department issued a Lutheran Church Directory every few years, providing a listing of all Lutheran congregations. Annually a summary of membership statistics for all the Lutheran bodies was compiled and published. An increasingly useful reference library was maintained, and a subject file that had 2,000 listings. An information service continued to be a main feature of this Department's tasks, with 60 inquiries a week coming by telephone and mail and personal visit from Lutherans and non-Lutherans on all aspects of Lutheran history and contemporary life. Many of these questions involved hours of research. Articles and other materials on Lutheranism were also prepared for a great variety of reference works. By means of a special project in 1964-1965 this Department, under the capable leadership of Helen M. Knubel, organized the Council's archives as the "Archives of Cooperative Lutheranism," in order to make accessible to historians and students the materials that tell the story of the NLC and its sister agencies. The Department of Research and Statistics was another effective instrument for spreading accurate information about Lutherans both within the denominational family and to the general public.

The *National Lutheran,* begun as a house organ in the 1930's to carry information about Council activities primarily to Lutheran pastors, became by degrees during this period (1953-1966) a magazine of broader Lutheran interest with feature articles and news columns that covered the whole range of religion, though the focus continued to be upon the activities of cooperative Lutheranism. Changes of format made for greater physical attractiveness as well. In 1954 this journal went on a subscription basis, though five of the participating bodies subscribed for their total list of pastors. Efforts were also made to expand the lay readership. By 1964 the subscription list exceeded 15,000. A quarterly in the mid-1940's, this journal expanded to become a bimonthly and then a monthly publication. Latterly the *LWA Bulletin,* informational materials for pastors on the work of Lutheran World Action, was issued four times a year as an insert in the *National Lutheran.* Editing these publications became virtually a full-time post, coupled with the editing of *A Mighty Fortress,* a four-page paper sent to about 80,000 men and women in military service by the NLC Bureau of Service to Military Personnel. For more than thirty-five years the *National Lutheran* played an increasingly effective role in Lutheran journalism as the interpreter and advocate of inter-Lutheran cooperation.

Representation at the nation's capital, begun as a staff position in 1948 under the Division of Public Relations, continued through this period with increased effectiveness as contacts and knowledge accumulated. Secretary Robert E. Van Deusen arranged appointments for Lutheran leaders with government officials, provided liaison with foreign Lutheran exchange visitors in Washington, attended conferences on national life, secured technical information for Lutheran leaders on a variety of subjects, expedited visa applications, made analyses and wrote releases about legislative matters, etc. Annually he carried major responsibility, in cooperation with the Lutheran Church–Missouri Synod, for the Washington Seminar for Lutheran Students and the Seminar on the Church and National Life, this latter conducted for Lutheran men and women in the federal government.

Representation in other areas of inter-religious and public life was also a major responsibility of the Division of Public Relations from its beginning in 1945. During the last few years a volunteer observer at the United Nations reported to the Council on major developments in that great international body and frequently interpreted the UN to Lutheran groups. Most of the representation, however, was done by the executive secretary of the Division or continued to be done (as it had before 1945) by the executive director of the Council. In two decades five men served as executive secretary for public relations—the Reverend Paul C. Empie (while he was Ralph Long's assistant), the Reverend Carl E. Lund-Quist, the Reverend Joseph Simonson, Harold E. Hammond, and the Reverend Philip A. Johnson. Johnson's report on the year 1963 illustrates this role by listing the conferences attended: [5]

> National Conference on Religion and Race, Chicago
> Radiation and Social Ethics, University of Chicago
> Ethics and Politics in World Affairs, Princeton Theological Seminary
> Church-State Consultations (2), Washington, D.C.
> Seminar, U.S. Committee for UNICEF, New York
> Institute on Human Relations, American Jewish Committee, New York
> Kirchentag, Dortmund, Germany (ecumenical visitor for NCCC)
> National Council of Churches Triennial Assembly, Philadelphia
> Religious Public Relations Council, Chicago
> National Lutheran Editors' and Managers' Association, Minneapolis
> Lutheran Broadcasters' Consultation (2), Minneapolis and New York
> Lutheran Foreign Missions Conference, St. Louis
> Church and National Life Seminar, Gettysburg
> Lutheran Students Seminar, Washington, D.C.

His regular committee and board assignments included:

> National Council of Churches; General Public Interpretations
> Committee, Broadcasting and Film Commission, Peace
> Corps Committee
> United Nations Church Representatives
> Protestant-Orthodox Center, New York World's Fair
> Program and Publicity, Lutheran Exhibit, New York World's
> Fair
> Contemporary Christian Art, Inc., New York

The Division of Public Relations accomplished a variety of other tasks for the Council, such as arrangements for a series of radio programs depicting various kinds of Lutheran campus ministry at universities, provision for an ongoing series of public relations workshops for the Lutherans of various areas, the Council's part in preparing for the 450th Anniversary of the Lutheran Reformation (1967) and the preparation of this history of cooperative Lutheranism and the NLC, *Lutherans in Concert.*

Welfare Gains

The Division of Welfare registered steady gains during its last fourteen years without making significant changes in program. In 1954 Clarence Krumbholz resigned after fifteen years as executive secretary, to be succeeded by the Reverend Henry J. Whiting, and in 1963 by the Reverend G. S. Thompson. Sensitive to trends in general welfare work, the Division gave more attention to the problems of the aging and their institutional care during the 1950's. It also sought to encourage the tendency on the part of local agencies and institutions that had been only loosely Lutheran in affiliation to seek closer ties with the churches themselves. For example, the Division developed a proposed constitution for the use of inter-Lutheran agencies that would be adaptable to the differing polities of the various Lutheran bodies. Increasingly study and planning were done in concert with the Department of Social Welfare of the Lutheran Church–Missouri Synod, while the Division also undertook to clarify its relationship to the national welfare offices of its own participating bodies.

A major facet of the Division's tasks was to conduct studies and surveys in the welfare field. This often eventuated in a brochure of information or guidelines or a printed or mimeographed report. There were several studies on trends in general welfare, a study on the role of Lutheran welfare in strengthening the family, one providing suggestions concerning the founding of Lutheran homes for the aged, a survey of Lutheran chaplaincy services at state institutions, a study on the roles of the church in serving the mentally retarded, a set of guidelines for Lutheran groups planning to establish a social welfare program, a study of the relation of church and state in welfare matters, etc.

Field studies and consultation services continued to be one of the largest avenues of the Division's staff services. In one year, for example, consultants made a study of a children's home in Buffalo, New York, a study of an old folks' home in South Carolina, and two studies of institutional relationships in Central Pennsylvania. Another year there was an investigation of an Arizona hospital and a study of the Lutheran welfare agencies and institutions in Ohio. In a third year consultative studies were made in Minneapolis, Saginaw (Michigan), Pittsburgh, and Baltimore. These field studies were a staple product of the Division and were aimed at upgrading the work of Lutherans in welfare.

With the same aim, recruitment of social welfare personnel was pursued steadily during these years. A college-agency liaison plan annually brought a score or more of social work representatives from Lutheran agencies to college campuses for "career days" of discussion with interested students. The national consultant in this program visited other Lutheran campuses as well as students in graduate schools of social work who had Lutheran scholarships. A brochure for college students and conferences for graduate students proved helpful in encouraging Lutheran youth to prepare for social welfare careers.

The Division of Welfare also prepared an annual *Lutheran Health and Welfare Directory*, listing 533 agencies in 1963, and a journal, the *National Lutheran Social Welfare Quarterly*. These editing responsibilities were part of the staff services provided by the Division for the National Lutheran Social Welfare Conference, a free conference of Lutheran individuals and organizations concerned with health and welfare activities. In addition, Division staff carried through the Conference's meetings which were national and regional in alternate years.

The Division of Welfare's work in cultivating Lutheran chaplaincy services developed along three lines. One was a consultation and survey service to Lutheran health and welfare agencies that maintain chaplaincy services. This work was similar to other consultative services offered by the Division. A second aspect was a liaison with United States government agencies in order to assure a spiritual ministry to Lutherans in Veterans Administration hospitals and federal prisons. In 1964 the secretary reported that there were 29 full-time chaplains, 45 part-time chaplains and 98 contact pastors ministering within the 171 VA hospitals. At the same time there were five full-time chaplains and 26 contact pastors ministering to Lutherans in the 33 federal prisons. Nearly half a million pieces of literature were distributed to these chaplains for their tasks. This work was coordinated with that of the Missouri Synod in the same field.

In 1962 a second secretary was secured to handle the third sphere of the Division's involvement in chaplaincy services, namely, clinical pastoral education. Here was an advance in cooperative Lutheran activity, reflecting the growing popularity and importance of specialized clinical experiences and training to prepare clergymen for pastoral care. This secretary worked in close conjunction with the theological seminaries, since clinical pastoral education (CPE) was viewed more and more as a significant adjunct to seminary courses. More than 200 Lutherans enrolled in CPE programs in the summer of 1965. But the Division's primary concern was the preparation of qualified chaplains for welfare institutions that were increasingly seeking full-time chaplains. Emphasis lay upon raising standards of Lutheran chaplaincy work. The main instrument was a process of supervising trainees and granting certificates of supervisory competence to these trainees when standards were fulfilled. An official document called "Criteria and Standards for Lutheran Clinical Pastoral Education" was developed and a standing committee supported the staff secretary by giving large segments of time to counseling trainees and granting accreditation. Accreditation gave official endorsement for a chaplain at a particular institution to become a supervisor of the training of other clergymen or seminarians. This CPE program for Lutherans paralleled two non-denominational CPE programs that were well established.

Immigrant Services

Assistance to refugees and other immigrants continued to be a major welfare concern of the NLC from 1953 to 1966. Lutheran Resettlement Service, set up by the Division of Welfare in 1948 in order to help refugees settle in the United States under a particular act of Congress, went out of existence in 1953 after that act expired. But a new program was set up at the same time as the Division's "Service to Immigrants." One aspect of the new program was aimed at helping the Lutherans among the regular flow of immigrants. On the subject of immigration this service represented Lutherans before the government and voluntary agencies, worked with the Lutheran World Federation in behalf of immigrants, provided services at points of entry as needed, referred incoming persons to congregations in the areas where they settled, gave information and counsel to Lutherans inquiring about the immigration of relatives or friends, coordinated Lutheran welfare services for immigrants, and helped to collect loans made by LWF or NLC for transportation or other purposes. In 1958 efforts were begun to develop a system of referral, beginning in Germany and Scandinavia, for incoming Lutherans in order to retain them in the fellowship of the church. It was estimated that 20,000 Lutherans came to the United States each year as regular quota immigrants.

Another part of the program begun in 1953 was called Lutheran Refugee Service. This service was provided as a response to a new act of Congress admitting refugees over a four-year period. Its duties were quite comparable to its predecessor, Lutheran Resettlement Service. But this time the Lutheran Church–Missouri Synod cooperated fully so that Lutheran Refugee Service was a joint Council-Missouri Synod enterprise into which a million dollars was put at a ratio of 70% from the Council and 30% from the Missouri Synod. After initial problems and uncertainties because of the complicated requirements of the law, the new LRS succeeded in bringing more than 15,000 refugees into the United States in the following four years. A staff of 28 was maintained in the national office and there were 35 full-time or part-time staff in area offices across the country. Thousands of other American Lutherans helped to secure assurances or provide other support for the program.

Because of the refugees who fled Hungary after the revolt of 1956, and for other reasons, Lutheran Refugee Service did not come to an end in 1957 as originally intended. However, in 1958 services to regular immigrants were reorganized and in 1960 the total program became Lutheran Immigration Service, a program jointly sponsored with the Lutheran Church–Missouri Synod. This brought the Missouri Synod into full partnership in a permanent program in the field of immigration. Residual responsibilities for the refugee programs included collection of payments on loans. It is evidence of the success of the refugee work and a testimony to the character of the resettled persons that in 1961 90% of all loans had been repaid. Major tasks of LIS involved counsel and information on immigration procedures, arrangement of reception services at points of entry, and representation of Lutheran churches before the government and voluntary agencies. The effective work of LIS in this last area (representation) will be discussed in the next chapter. In cooperation with the Lutheran World Federation and many other Lutheran organizations LIS gave some kind of assistance to about three thousand immigrants each year. For three years in the 1960's LIS assisted more than 1,600 Cuban refugees in Miami, Florida. This was largely welfare work, including distribution of food and clothing, counseling and job assistance for people with no Lutheran backgrounds.

In summing up the significance of cooperative Lutheran programs for refugees and other immigrants one would stress the international aid for brethren in the faith and the thousands of lives for whom a new and hopeful start was provided. However, from the standpoint of inter-Lutheran cooperation and unity, Donald E. Anderson, director of LIS, made these perceptive comments:

In the era since the last war we have assisted Lutherans from Germany, Latvia, Lithuania, Estonia, Czechoslovakia, Rumania, Poland, as well as others. We have assisted well over 70,000 who have established themselves in the United States through thousands of local congregations and parishes. Norwegians received Germans, Swedes received Latvians, the Danes received Hungarians and the Germans received Poles. These refugees and immigrants became integrated with our congregations in America and literally proved beyond any doubt that nationality lines could be crossed easily and effectively.

Noting that the new immigrants contrasted with earlier ethnic groups of Lutheran newcomers to America because they did not establish their own national church bodies, Anderson pointed to the way these people both enriched Lutheran diversity and contributed to Lutheran unity:

In fact, the overwhelming testimony from pastors of all Churches has been that these people strengthen their congregations and congregational life. Thus, the refugees were the forerunners and contributed greatly, in my opinion, to the breaking down of nationality lines that had separated our Lutheran Churches in America for so long.[6]

Without doubt the cooperative Lutheran resettlement programs contributed greatly to the achievement of this desirable result.

Changes in Campus Ministry

During its last fourteen years the Division of College and University Work continued along the lines described in the previous chapter. Not that it was a static program. On the contrary, it was one of the most lively aspects of Council work, registering considerable growth and showing sensitivity to the changing moods, intellectual currents, and needs at the nation's colleges and universities.

As the student population spiraled upward during these years the DCUW was hard put to it to keep up with its growing constituency. In 1965 there were 78 clergymen serving on the staff as campus pastors and eight more on the national staff, under the direction of the Reverend A. Henry Hetland, who had become executive secretary in 1959. There were 35 full-time lay associates, nine seminary interns doing full-time campus ministry and twelve part-time assistants. Also involved were about 525 contact pastors. These people gave service at about a thousand colleges and universities. That same year the total operating budget exceeded $1.75 million with $660,000 of this in the national budget from the participating bodies. Estimates placed the total number of contacts as follows:

Worship led by professional staff	20,000
Worship led by contact pastors	100,000
Formal teaching	20,000
Informal teaching and discussion	30,000
Serious counselling	6,000
Work with foreign students	1,500
Personal work with faculty	1,000
Various student movement meetings	50,000
Retreats	15,000

The emphasis of the DCUW continued to broaden beyond student work to encompass a ministry to the entire campus and every aspect of the university community. The task of the Division was defined as "to assist the community of Jesus Christ to fulfill its vocation in the academic world." Thus the staff continued to make special efforts to reach faculty people, and the Division continued to support several chairs of religion at state universities. A ministry was developed to meet the particular needs of foreign students and to draw them into campus religious activities. New efforts were launched to minister to the ever-increasing number of married students in a manner suitable to their changed circumstance. It became recognized procedure to include the commuting student in a campus ministry rather than assuming that he would maintain home church ties. The DCUW took a larger and more direct part in recruitment for the ministry and other church vocations as it became clear that a larger percentage of seminarians were coming from non-church schools. In 1959 the Division staff reported names of 630 students who were preparing for church occupations and were in touch with staff personnel.

Preaching and the sacraments were increasingly made the focus of campus ministry. During the 1950's and the 1960's students were less inclined to seek social and recreational opportunities in their religious groups. Interest in discussion groups continued, and there was an increased seriousness about course work in religion whether for credit or not. Stress was put upon evangelism and the student responsibility to witness. And attendance at worship services increased, particularly when the services were held at student centers or on the campus. Such campus ministry extension centers were 28 in number in 1965 and the trend was toward their increase as the most effective way to reach students with the Word and sacraments. Experimental forms of liturgy frequently emerged from the campus ministry, indicating ferment in ways of worship and a dissatisfaction with older patterns. *Oremus,* a book of worship issued by the LSAA, became popular in student groups.

Student centers continued to be built at a steady pace with the funds contributed by the Council's participating bodies and their constituent units in the area where a particular project was located. In the 1947-54 period $960,000 was spent on 36 projects; in 1955-60 a total of $1.6 million was invested in 37 projects; and in 1961-65 allocations of $1.9 million were made for 63 projects. Virtually all these buildings were secured with the help of some Lutheran Student Foundation, typically an incorporated organization operating on a local area or state level, through which representatives of constituent units of participating bodies supported all aspects of the local campus ministry and became the property-holders for the centers. Whatever the changes in the philosophy of a campus ministry, the facilities of a student center and the support of a Student Foundation remained central to the operation.

As in other branches of the church's life, however, it became increasingly important that the student center and the whole program be wisely and closely related to the ecumenical or interdenominational aspects of campus ministry. The relation of Lutherans to other religious groups on campus has been a complex and ever-changing one. The Division's early years coincided with a time of consolidation of a distinctly Lutheran thrust and the emphasis on Word and sacraments was uniquely Lutheran. But by the 1960's it was quite clear that, without watering down this Lutheran ministry, the context was such that the religious or at least the Christian forces had to work together at certain specific tasks. An ecumenical approach to foreign students became an imperative. In relating to social action programs and social protest movements religious groups found it strategic to move in concert at many points. It was deemed preferable for Lutheran offices to be within general religious buildings. The DCUW joined the National Student Christian Federation in 1961. These are illustrations of a trend.

The international context also became more important for college and university work. Large numbers of foreign students were one factor. Easier transportation made attendance at international student conferences a more popular activity. A Division-sponsored European study-work project for a select group of Americans every few years helped to broaden horizons of outstanding Lutheran young people. In 1964 this overseas project was held in Latin America. The most important influence was that higher education itself became international-minded in a variety of ways that made an impact on students and professors. For the DCUW itself this meant an increased interest in exchange programs and closer ties to the Lutheran World Federation.

In its twenty years the campus ministry of the National Lutheran Council carried through a distinguished service for American Lutheranism in a difficult setting. The staff consistently operated at a high level of morale, and, indeed, were considered something of an elite among the church's servants, though university campuses were often forbidding places in which to offer the ministrations of the Christian faith. Students and their campus Christian leaders were frequently at odds with church officials on many issues of their faith. Certainly, campus Lutherans were impatient with the separations among Lutheran bodies. In general the DCUW did a fine job in ministering to students within the structures of the organized churches. And campus experiences of inter-Lutheran friendships and joint activities made a strong contribution to cooperative Lutheranism, the effects of which are accumulating as successive generations of students enter into adult church life.

Services to Military Personnel

The Council's Bureau of Service to Military Personnel was established in 1948 under the leadership of the Reverend Gynther Storaasli. As the postwar and peacetime agency for NLC Lutherans it coordinated the relationships between the participating bodies, their chaplains in the armed services, and the government. Its work has been efficient and valuable but not spectacular.

In serving the church bodies the Bureau transmitted information on procurement programs and policy changes in regard to chaplains. It served as the clearing agency for the endorsement of clergymen as chaplains, assumed responsibility for the Lutheran quota coverage, and forwarded to endorsing agencies of church bodies the monthly reports of the chaplains.

As its service to the chaplains on active duty, the Bureau maintained contacts through monthly reports, correspondence, official visits, conferences, and news bulletins, and provided religious tracts and pamphlets in large quantities for free distribution to military personnel.

Over the years the Bureau's program expanded to include retreats for chaplains, both overseas and in the United States, a bulletin sent directly to Lutheran military personnel called *A Mighty Fortress,* and representation of the chaplaincy at seminaries and elsewhere in the life of the church. A pre-induction booklet was prepared and distributed. A program of contact pastors adjacent to military installations was developed, and a congregational follow-up program for keeping in touch with military personnel. In recognition of its enlarged role the Bureau was accorded Division status in 1964. For its last thirteen years this whole program was in charge of the Reverend Engebret O. Midboe.

To provide Lutheran service centers for off-duty military personnel, the Lutheran Service Commission was created in 1951. Quite similar to the undertaking by the same name which had flourished during World War II and had been phased out in 1948, this new LSC differed in that it represented full cooperation in one agency for the Bureau of Service to Military Personnel of the NLC and the Armed Services Commission of the Lutheran Church–Missouri Synod. In this connection it was agreed that no Lutheran serviceman would be denied the Lord's Supper because of his synodical affiliation—an agreement which has done much to facilitate friendly relations and fruitful cooperation in recent decades. Reflecting the nation's mobilization for the Korean War, the LSC had a dozen clergymen and more than two dozen salaried laymen on its staff within two years, operating 45 parish centers and service centers.

By 1955 the LSC domestic program was being curtailed somewhat and the emphasis switched to overseas service centers at places where there were semipermanent military installations involving large numbers of United States personnel. This aspect of the program continued to grow. The domestic centers were not discontinued but came under considerable discussion as some people disputed their value during peacetime. In 1965 the LSC was operating ten domestic centers and six overseas ones, as well as giving financial support to twenty-one parish programs in this field, reporting total center attendance of about 400,000 annually. In later years, with the increase of small, isolated military units, the Commission gave attention to ways of reaching these men through "circuit riders," contact pastors, literature, etc. The NLC executive in the Commission's work was the Reverend Carl F. Yaeger.

These programs for military personnel fostered inter-Lutheran friendship and understanding on many levels. Particularly the Commission, with its broadly inter-Lutheran local committees that in many areas provided oversight for the work of a given center, played an important role in the *rapprochement* of America's Lutherans.

Large, Broad, Diversified

The broad summaries of major programs which have constituted this chapter show how, between 1953 and the Council's termination, the National Lutheran Council effectively served as the cooperative agency for American Lutheran mission, large in volume, broad in scope, diversified in outreach.

Other programs and the changed context which affected all Council activity in the latter half of this period will provide the focus of the next chapter.

IX | The Changing Landscape (1959-1966)

In its last years the National Lutheran Council took several significant new turns that reflected radically altered circumstances. Some of them were the result of progress toward consolidation of the Lutheran forces of America. As such they were in part the product of the Council's own achievements. Others, more subtle and more significant, were responses to the large forces that were shaping the whole twentieth century. They carried the thrust of the Gospel as Lutherans sought to apply it to the needs of modern man.

Search for New Cooperative Patterns

When the 1950's got underway it became clear that there would be mergers among the Council's participating bodies but not one merger to include all the bodies. This failure (or it could be considered a limited success) was a source of frustration to many people. It could have been a factor inhibiting the increase of inter-Lutheran cooperation, though the previous chapter has shown that cooperative activity did not wither.

At any rate, two church bodies emerged where there had been eight. In 1960 The American Lutheran Church was created by the merger of the American Lutheran Church (formed in 1930), the Evangelical Lutheran Church (formerly the Norwegian Lutheran Church of America), the United Evangelical Lutheran Church, and the Lutheran Free Church. In 1962 the Lutheran Church in America was created by merger of the Augustana Lutheran Church, the United Lutheran Church in America, the American Evangelical Lutheran Church, and the Suomi Synod.

This major development put a solemn question mark over the Council's whole life in the late 1950's. What would be the Council's role when there were only two participating bodies? Without the necessity for reaching consensus among eight participants would the Council's rather elaborate machinery be unnecessary as the new ALC and LCA reached unilateral agreements? There was even the question whether two bodies might choose to go their separate ways, where eight smaller ones had felt the need for each other. The NLC's morale suffered under this uncertainty.

Broadly speaking, two factors led American Lutherans to continue their conciliar pattern as the major device for cooperative action on many fronts. One was the National Lutheran Council's own successful record, high reputation, symbolic meaning, and continuing efficient staff and machinery. The second factor was the context in which American church life found itself. In our introductory chapter we characterized the twentieth century as the age of ecumenism and pluralism. These influences made themselves felt as obviously predominating forces in the 1950's and 1960's. And it also became clear that he who affirms ecumenism and pluralism must also affirm conciliarism.

As it turned out, the crucial decision was made by the Lutheran Church–Missouri Synod. Its decision to participate in a successor to the NLC undoubtedly was influenced by the two factors mentioned. A look at its relation to the NLC indicates this.

As early as the wartime emergencies of the 1940's the Missouri Lutherans found themselves under considerable compulsion to cooperate if they were to participate in the mainstream of church responsibilities. In the handling of orphaned missions, for example, governments looked to the International Missionary Council or the Lutheran World Federation. Similarly refugee resettlement had to be done cooperatively. Missourians were reluctant to extend official cooperation where complete doctrinal agreement was lacking. Often they agreed simply to unofficial coordination or to cooperation on the part of one particular board or agency but not of the Lutheran Church–Missouri Synod itself. Yet cooperative activity on both local and national levels slowly increased. And there was a positive response. Seldom was the relationship severed after it was once established. Council people formed warm friendships with Missouri Lutherans. Three joint agencies—Lutheran World Relief, the Lutheran Service Commission, and Lutheran Immigration Service—provided formal ties. In nearly every major area of the Council's work there was at least some recognized cooperative activity with Missouri Synod people. Mutual trust was building up. Faced by the necessity of forming new relationships with a friendlier Roman Catholicism, confronted by an increasingly secularized nation, caught in a world of population explosions and angry, self-conscious have-not peoples, Missouri Lutherans were more ready to recognize NLC Lutherans as fellow Lutherans. Differences of theology and church practice were not to be ignored, but they became matters for serious intramural discussion rather than separating barriers.

Formation of LCUSA

In 1958 Paul Empie, keenly aware of the changes outlined above, used his report to the Council's annual meeting to make a spirited appeal for reappraisal of the patterns of Lutheran cooperation "in the light of contemporary ecclesiastical and international developments." The history of the NLC, he asserted, "is in a sense merely the record of developing acceptance of each other by Lutheran groups in America, resulting in increasing cooperative relationships over a forty year period." One lesson learned, he added, was that, whereas Lutherans do not form organic union without careful doctrinal agreement, "the degree of cooperation achieved from time to time came about largely as a result of the pressures of national and international events." Factors delaying cooperation were practical rather than theological. Since we are presently, he claimed, operating with a framework geared to the world of 1945, we must ask searchingly: "Is not the situation of World War II and its aftermath already a closed chapter of history, with a new stage well underway?"[1] Empie proposed an NLC-sponsored conference for 1959, which would implement for the first time the Council's constitutional provision that: "The Council may convene general conferences of representatives of the Participating Bodies, for the study and discussion of practical problems." He suggested that non-Council Lutherans be invited to participate as observers.

The councillors acted on this proposal, inviting non-Council Lutherans to full participation in the discussion of patterns of cooperation. At first the Missouri Synod declined the offer, but when Empie gave assurance that doctrinal discussions relating to cooperation among Christians would be part of the agenda, Missouri agreed in June of 1959 to participate. In 1960 and 1961 three consultations were held on "The Unity of the Gospel," "The Significance of Confessional Subscription," and "What Kind of Cooperation Is Possible in View of Discussions to Date?" Enough doctrinal consensus emerged to project a new cooperative agency to replace the National Lutheran Council and to include the Lutheran Church–Missouri Synod. Other Lutheran groups were again invited to participate, and the ALC, LCA, and Missouri Synod were joined by the small Synod of Evangelical Lutheran Churches during the three years of planning. In 1964-66 the four church bodies accepted the proposed constitution and on January 1, 1967, there came into being the Lutheran Council in the United States of America, a cooperative agency which included 95% of the Lutherans.

The new agency had a twofold purpose, namely, theological discussion and cooperation in specified areas of Christian service. All participating bodies were required to take part in the theological discussion in order "to seek to achieve theological consensus in a systematic and continuing way." Each body could elect to participate in other areas of activity or to abstain. This stress upon the theological discussion was a concession to the Missouri Synod on the part of the NLC bodies, which had avoided doctrinal discussions in connection with council cooperation since 1920. It was a turning point and a concession for the Missouri Synod, on the other hand, to agree to organized associations with other Lutherans while doctrinal differences remained.

Here was a real breakthrough in approaches to Lutheran unity and union as well as a significant forward step in Lutheran cooperation.

The formation of the LCUSA meant the end of the National Lutheran Council and marks the terminal point for this narrative. In a sense it was also the metamorphosis of the older Council into a more inclusive agency, with the Missourians fully in it and theological discussions fully a part of it. The functions of the new organization as stated in its constitution had a familiar ring to the student of NLC history.

On the other hand, there were some serious drawbacks to the new arrangements. Some programs were cut back. There were, for example, no provisions for the comity agreements in American missions to provide for careful cooperation in the location of new congregations. And it took three separate organizations to continue the NLC's tasks. Missouri Lutherans were not ready to commit their college and university ministry to a cooperative venture, so LCUSA's educational duties were limited to the co-ordinating role, whereas the cooperative campus ministry of the ALC and the LCA became a separate entity, the National Lutheran Campus Ministry. Since Missouri and the Synod of Evangelical Lutheran Churches did not belong to the Lutheran World Federation, the U.S.A. National Committee of the Lutheran World Federation became a separate organization through which the ALC and the LCA cooperated in their international outreach. Legally, this organization continued the NLC, so that technically the NLC did not die in 1967, but simply limited itself to its international aspects. Close cooperation between LCUSA and the U.S.A. National Committee was assumed in arrangements for adjoining facilities in New York City and for the sharing of some staff services.

During its last seven or eight years conjectures and plans for the new organizations set the atmosphere for the NLC's work. This inhibited long-range planning and precluded any large-scale venturing into new territory. Many of the staff left the Council, though a large percentage found their way into the new organizations. On the other hand, this ending for the Council provided a hopeful note, since the work was mostly being continued, and brought a sense of success for the NLC itself, since three successor organizations would carry an enhanced role for cooperative Lutheran activities. Furthermore, there was much carry-over in procedure and personnel with a careful meshing of the shifting gears. In Empie's comparison the change was "that of one runner in a relay race transferring the baton to another—at the moment of transfer both are running!" [2]

Age of Dialogue

Meanwhile, the larger context and atmosphere of the modern world shaped all this conciliar history in fundamental ways which found expression in the life of the National Lutheran Council during its final years. If one wished to characterize the whole age in one word, it would be "dialogue." In the 1960's American Lutherans were clearly caught up in the Age of Dialogue. They lived in one tight little world, geographically and technologically speaking, in which people with widely divergent ideas and experiences jostled one another. Radically one world, radically pluralistic. Modern humanity was thrust into synthetic and uneasy togetherness, many worlds intersecting, many values crisscrossing, many idealogies competing, many peoples mixing. As the means of communication multiplied, the thought worlds divided and clashed. It became desperately important for people—the alternative was annihilation—to reach out to meet and understand people very different from themselves. It was a time of the proliferation of dialogues.

By dialogue is meant the discussion or sharing of experiences between diverse individuals or between differing groups in which each partner seeks to understand the others at a deep level and is open and willing to be shaped himself to some serious extent by the others and by their common quest. The age of dialogue did not begin in 1960. In fact, the whole history of the NLC reflects the situation in which American Lutherans were thrust into many dialogues. But by 1960 the process had gone so far that a new stage was reached in which modern men became more self-conscious about these encounters and more committed to structures for dialogue.

Exchange Programs

One obvious example of the way in which the new atmosphere of dialogue penetrated the NLC's activities was its exchange programs. Emerging at various points in the Council's organization, often directed toward a study opportunity for young Lutherans, these programs had dialogue as a main purpose, introducing people to each other across oceans, across national boundaries, across a variety of cultural gaps. The study-work projects of the Division of College and University Work, mentioned in the previous chapter, are an example.

In 1957 a staff person was engaged to handle in one office the various exchanges getting underway, since it had become clear at the Minneapolis Assembly of the LWF that year that exchange of persons was to increase rapidly. There were three main exchange programs during the Council's last decade. One, sponsored by the Department of World Service of the LWF, was called the Church Workers Exchange. It provided for three-month study and observation assignments for pastors and lay-workers in a country other than their own, giving them opportunity to observe some aspect of church life particularly relevant to their own ministry. In a decade 194 people from all over the world came to the United States on this program and just over a hundred Americans went overseas, mostly to Germany or Scandinavia. There were, of course, exchanges that did not involve Americans or the NLC at all.

A second exchange program, connected with the NLC and LWF work in world missions, in a decade brought 109 people—72 of them from Tanzania—to the United States for two years of study as candidates for bachelor's degrees, theological degrees, or other advanced degrees. These young people were helped toward a better education in areas of specialization for which training was unavailable or poor in their homeland. They were expected to return to their homeland to serve.

The third exchange program, the earliest to get underway, was in the field of theological education, sponsored by the Council and Federation agencies charged with theological concerns. In the Council's last decade about 65 students had come to the

United States and about 42 had gone from this country to Europe, the latter nearly all seeking doctorates in theology.

Many other visitors from overseas were assisted by Council staff in developing itineraries and in other ways. This whole exchange not only helped to prepare many young people for effective service. It also served to promote international understanding and to create a sense of international community among Lutherans.

Theological Dialogues

The Department of Theological Cooperation of the Council, being mainly the American agent for the Department of Theology of the LWF, gave itself in the 1950's primarily to exchange work and conferences featuring European theologians. In the 1960's it started to play a larger role. For a time of dialogues Lutherans needed a common voice and started to turn to the Council to provide that agency. In so doing they were reflecting two other specific trends of the times. One was the broadening of the ecumenical movement to bring an almost massive effort for Christians to meet and understand fellow Christians across the barriers that had divided Protestant, Roman Catholic, and Orthodox churchmen. This was an international phenomenon. On the American scene a second significant trend led councils of churches into theological discussions on the national, regional, and local levels, even involving many laymen in their homes in "livingroom dialogues." Like the National Lutheran Council, interdenominational councils of churches had emerged and flourished in the early decades of the twentieth century by tacitly avoiding theological discussion as potentially divisive. After the mid-century it became fashionable in the name of dialogue to bring one's theological concerns directly into his ecumenical programs.

Actually, the Department of Theological Cooperation only made the barest beginnings in fostering theological exchange among its participating bodies. By 1960 it was serving the seminaries of its constituency by planning lecture tours of European theologians from school to school. At about the same time it began theological conferences for the younger theologians of its participating bodies. It also secured authorization to undertake specific studies at the request of one or more of its church bodies, but little of this was actually accomplished. This kind of activity, however, fed into the projected theological programs of the successor council, LCUSA.

The significant breakthrough in theological discussion came in the call to provide a Lutheran voice in dialogue with other denominations. In 1961 the National Lutheran Council itself (as the U.S.A. National Committee of the Lutheran World Federation) was invited to engage in doctrinal discussions with the North American Area of the World Alliance of Reformed Churches Holding the Presbyterian Order. The purpose was to determine to what extent differences which had divided these communions in the past still constituted obstacles to mutual understanding. By invitation the Lutheran Church–Missouri Synod agreed to participate in the ensuing conversations. After a preliminary exploration in 1962, a panel of theologians—Lutheran and Reformed—met annually for three years to discuss prepared papers on major doctrines about which there had traditionally been disagreement. The papers and group conclusions were published as a book, *Marburg Revisited.* In an evaluation meeting in 1966 the theologians who had participated in discussion declared that they had found no "insuperable obstacles to pulpit and altar fellowship."

Beginnings of similar conversations with Roman Catholics were made in 1965 and with the Orthodox in 1966. In these dialogues the pattern of annual theological conferences, with Missourians included, appeared quite similar to those with the Reformed theologians. The NLC's successors became responsible for continuing this work.

An Altered International Outreach

In equally significant ways an altered context brought changes in the whole international outreach of the Council. The ecumenical dimension became more pronounced in programs for relief, interchurch aid, and refugees. In 1954 the Council gave $100,000 to the work of non-Lutheran agencies, notably Church World Service, the world YMCA, the American Bible Society, and particular projects of the National Council of Churches and the World Council of Churches. By 1959 this amount had increased to a quarter of a million dollars. The perennial question of how to relate to interdenominational organizations found expression in a statement adopted by the councillors in 1959 called "Planning Together With Other Protestants." In that same year Lutheran World Relief posed as one of its major questions: "What is the role of LWR as a confessional agency in the context of ecumenical relationships?" In 1964-65 the Department of World Service, LWF, at the request of the World Council of Churches and with money from the Lutherans of several nations, established the Tanganyika Christian Refugee Service to settle in that land refugees coming over three border areas from Mozambique, the Congo, and Ruanda. This work took close cooperation with the Tanzania Council of Churches and the United Nations High Commissioner for Refugees. These are examples of the widespread and increasing ecumenical involvement.

A more basic shift in underlying principles is discernible in these and similar events. Indicative of the changed mood is the fact that Lutheran World Relief started to ask fundamental questions about its operations and became inevitably caught up in difficult judgments that had theological overtones. Thus an organization that had been founded to carry through external and material acts of mercy for Lutherans, with co-sponsorship by the appropriate arm of the Lutheran Church–Missouri Synod and some cooperation by Lutherans of the still more conservative Wisconsin Synod, found itself confronted by some of the deepest problems of human existence.

Both LWR and the Department of Lutheran World Service in its allocation of Lutheran World Action funds found that the need for their programs was endless. As needs lessened in Europe by 1955, more materials were sent to Asia and Africa. Rising populations and teeming millions always on the brink of starvation and at subhuman levels of existence raised sharply the question of the best use of limited programs of aid. Should LWR extend help in situations of endemic need? How far can LWR go in accepting subsidies from government? LWR and the Department of World Service shifted their emphasis to self-help programs that would draw out local initiative and multiply local resources at the places of need. This involved common study and planning with many other agencies. It involved an LWR grant, for example, to Korea Church World Service for the training of Christian social workers who would go into the homes to minister to the needy and distressed. Relationships had to be worked out with governments, with indigenous churches, with the LWF, with ecumenical agencies, and with organizations such as the Red Cross.

Addressing itself to the root causes of hunger, LWR came to stress community development as the way to get at the basic problem. Self-help and community development projects included animal husbandry, land restoration, demonstration farms, building of roads, reservoirs, dams, wells, and establishment of community centers. Comparable was the responsibility of the National Lutheran Council for administering sizeable Ford Foundation grants (exceeding $800,000) to develop a Faculty of Economics at Nommensen University in Indonesia.

The NLC's international involvement was a complex operation, including very diverse activities in concert with a variety of people and organizations. It reflected a deep and stable commitment by American Lutherans to a cooperative overseas witness and service. Paul Empie once observed that

> after World War I the Lutheran churches in the U.S. rapidly completed the process of full entrance into American life; after World War II they ventured past the point of no return with respect to their involvements in the international arena.[3]

In the Council's last years it became a puzzling question how to spend wisely in the name of the Gospel the available money, men, and material. There was no question of withdrawal. But the philosophy of giving changed subtly. In previous years the particular causes had been fairly obvious and nearly always involved help for Lutheran brethren. Now aid programs had to be more selective, more imaginative, more creative. And they were more dialogic, i.e., they were aimed at stirring a response, starting a give-and-take, evoking hope and self-help among peoples who were often not Lutherans and in programs that were more economics than religion. To a larger extent American Lutherans were doing these things as their contribution to a world of swirling turmoil in which all peoples were being cast into a common destiny.

A Voice in National Policies

This same significant shift was manifested in the Council's domestic concerns, particularly in its renewed approach to broad reaches of the nation's public life. In the NLC's early days its public pronouncements and its representations before government were those of a minority group intent upon justifying themselves before the majority, establishing their loyalty to the American nation, and protecting their own interests at every point. Lutherans, of course, have never given up efforts to protect their denominational or institutional interests. But in its last years the Council began to develop a fresh voice on public issues. Still a minority, Lutherans were more relaxed and self-confident, more aware that public life consisted of many such minority voices and that Lutherans could say something helpful in the shaping of an evolving consensus at many points in public life.

Such a shift in approach to Council tasks reflected the whole of American Lutheran experience for five decades, what Empie called "full entrance into American life." The Council itself had been a major factor in channeling and shaping that experience of Lutherans vis-à-vis the American public, but it was a much broader experience involving hosts of laymen in their daily lives. There would be value in a study that traced these changes through the Council's pronouncements on social and public issues for nearly fifty years.

At the end of World War I, Council statements were concerned to say that Lutherans were full-fledged Americans and not simply transplanted Germans. The next general phase in the Council's pronouncements came in the 1930's when a Social Trends Committee became prominent in its life. Careful studies were developed and promulgated in a variety of ways. On such subjects as clean movies, the liquor problem, Communism, marriage and divorce, and gambling, these studies evidenced a real Lutheran concern for social issues and tended to provide moral judgments upon American society in keeping with traditional Lutheran ethical principles. This committee became absorbed in the more specific problems of Lutheran welfare institutions in the 1940's. During and after World War II public pronouncements were rather incidental to the Council's tasks, not receiving concerted attention. Like those of other denominations, the NLC's statements on war were balanced between condemnations of war and admissions of war's painful necessity, coupled with assertions of loyalty to the government. From the end of World War II until about 1957 the Council seldom sought the role of Lutheran spokesman on public issues, except through the Washington office and personal contacts.

In 1957 a new Social Trends Committee was established as a standing committee. As a result of its efforts the councillors adopted at the 1958 annual meeting a strong statement on human relations which was transmitted to the participating bodies for their use. This statement was reaffirmed and strengthened in 1964. In 1959 the councillors approved a detailed statement entitled "Toward a Statement of National Policy" as a Christian contribution to the current public discussion about definitions of the "national interest." An enlarged and enhanced Social Trends Committee was developing a number of studies and statements for Council adoption, many of them dealing with the complex relationships of church and state at points affecting NLC programs. In 1960, to give a partial listing, NLC resolutions favored a well thought-out and purposeful program of foreign aid; warned against federal aid to private schools on elementary and secondary levels; urged strong participation by the United States government in the World Refugee Year activities; and deplored recent acts of anti-Semitism. The next year a statement was adopted on "Religious Faith as a Factor in American Elections," and approval was given to a study on "Church Hospitals and the Hill-Burton Act." A year later the Council reaffirmed its 1951 expression of confidence in the useful role of the United Nations and took a positive stand regarding the U.S. Peace Corps. In 1963 a lengthy study on "Use of Public Tax Funds for Non-Public Schools" was discussed but was found to deal with too controversial a topic to be adopted. During its last three years pre-occupation with the structural changes proposed for Lutheran cooperation kept the Council from aggressive consideration of public issues.

These statements and studies represented a major effort on the part of the Council. In behalf of American Lutheranism the NLC sought to address helpfully some of the crucial issues that were arousing lively dialogues within the national life. A few of the statements received a wide hearing beyond Lutheran circles. The procedure of study, adoption, and commendation to the participating bodies was also an effort to develop a consensus among Lutherans on these complex and important public subjects. In both of its aspects—public and inter-Lutheran—this undertaking illustrates the changed role which the Council was adopting in the age of dialogue.

One could not claim, however, that these pronouncements and papers wielded great influence. That is always hard to determine. There is little evidence that Council positions were widely discussed among the general run of Lutherans or, for example, that they received extensive coverage in the daily newspapers. And NLC people were the first to recognize that methods had not been developed to provide a consensus that would speak for the mass of Lutherans with a united voice on important social issues in a manner to secure wide public attention. It was rather that a significant beginning had been made.

Immigration Legislation

At one point, namely, immigration legislation, Lutherans did, however, perform a notable public service—in concert with many other groups, of course.

Over the years the National Lutheran Council and related organizations had had a varied and distinguished record in bringing immigrants into the United States. Its staff had built up a large store of experience. From time to time representation on behalf of immigrants and of specific immigration policies had been made before government officials and legislators. Beginning in 1956 and in keeping with the changed policies reflected in the work of the Social Trends Committee, repeated efforts were made to help in securing more just and humane immigration legislation and the repeal of the national origins quota system. Council officials testified at a number of legislative hearings and issued at least eight papers publicizing their viewpoint. Year after year the councillors included this cause in resolutions they adopted, asking the federal government to establish non-discriminating immigration policies. In 1960 the Council approved a notable statement—later paralleled by a Missouri Synod statement—with the following concluding section: [4]

POSSIBLE OBJECTIVES OF U.S. IMMIGRATION LAWS

1. To supply our permanent population with a steady proportion of newcomers who have chosen the United States as their new homeland and who can impart to their American neighbors an understanding of the cultures, attitudes, and interests of other races and peoples of the world.
2. To assume the United States' proper share of international responsibility for the resettlement of refugees and of other persons urgently in need of the compassionate haven of a new homeland.
3. To facilitate the reuniting of families.
4. To facilitate the entry of persons possessing special skills or other capacities needed by the American economy and culture.
5. To admit annually a reasonable number of the persons described above on an objective basis of selection which, while discriminating, will not be discriminatory with respect to race, national origin, color, or religion, testifying thereby to the United States' recognition of the interlocking and mutual interests of all nations with regard to the migration of peoples, the interaction of cultures and the respect of universal human rights.

After years of continued agitation, along with a number of other agencies, Lutheran Immigration Service was able to report that 1965 legislation had upset the old quota system and had made possible the fulfillment of all five of the above objectives. There was evidence that the Lutheran testimony had been an influential one in this accomplishment.

The Council's role in immigration legislation indicated a notable turn of events for another reason. The position taken was a right-about-face from the stand of NLC leaders in 1928 and 1929. At that time the Council had objected to immigration laws because they did not have larger quotas for predominantly Lutheran countries. In the 1960's Lutherans in the name of justice, a diversified America, and humane national policy favored laws which reduced opportunities for immigration from predominantly Lutheran lands. Clearly this was action motivated by concern for the public welfare and for international good will. And Lutheran testimony had carried real weight precisely because that motivation was evident.

Lively Seeds

In the Council's dying years it is impressive to observe how many and how widely spread were its lively seeds. Three organizations sprang from its burial soil practically pre-matured, one of them, LCUSA, richly more inclusive in constituency. And during those final years the National Lutheran Council was able to enter into many places of the world's struggles and many areas of the world's ferment: training leaders for the indigenous church and young nation of Tanzania; strengthening the economics department of an Indonesian university; resettling refugees from the Congo; attacking the roots of poverty and hunger with dams and roads; training case workers for an ecumenical project in Korea; revising American immigration policy; debating American foreign policy and the use of tax monies for church relief programs or private schools; supporting the teaching of religion at state universities; providing television entertainment for children; and many more instances.

In an age of dialogue Lutherans were learning to take their part. As they did so they were discovering how much they belonged together and how much more they could accomplish cooperatively. It was not a simple success story, for there were many hesitancies and many opportunities were lost. But it was a story of encouraging progress. And it pointed toward larger accomplishments in prospect.

X

The Larger Meaning

Taking Stock

Spanning nearly half a century (1918-1966), the National Lutheran Council proved to be a durable agency for the channeling of cooperative activities by about two-thirds of America's Lutherans. The preceding chapters describe a vast volume of church work carried through by this agency. Yet a single book cannot begin to relate the human interest stories, the record of pioneer services, the fabric of the day-by-day response to human need in so many areas. Nor can these pages even touch upon the commitment, the often heroic dedication of dozens and hundreds of Christian men and women who have served God and their fellowmen in ways both glamorous and prosaic through the Council's manifold activities. In future years the Council's archives will remain a rich source from which historians can draw a more complete description of its operations and the drama inherent in much of it.

What does it all mean? Deeds of service done in Christ's name have their own inherent value, since the cup of cold water casts its shadow onto the very scene of the Last Judgment. But the historian notes some other meanings in this story of cooperative Lutheranism in twentieth century America.

185

Obviously many American Lutherans have for some decades been saying with conviction: We should be doing things together. As this conviction found expression it deepened and spread to others and increased its stream of common traffic. First it was public relations and overseas relief. Then welfare work was added, and university services, and urban planning, and theological discussion with the Reformed and the Roman Catholics. Slowly a hesitant Iowa Synod was included in the Council and finally the Lutheran Church–Missouri Synod became a partner in the successor council, LCUSA. Meanwhile, through the decades many Lutherans who were not fully a part of the Council persisted in maintaining some relationship—often tenuous, often tortuous—with the Council's programs. Why was this? Because the Council was the chief embodiment of a significant movement. Because cooperative action had a powerful appeal for Lutherans as they faced their twentieth century tasks. Lutherans sensed deeply, despite many obstacles and hindrances, that they should be doing things together by the very compulsions of the Gospel.

That is to say, there was a strong will to unity and a strong will toward outgoing mission, and these two thrusts created a movement of major proportions. In the early years of the century many informal and limited-purpose associations among Lutherans surrounded and nurtured the budding Council. By the middle of the century the burgeoning Council was supporting these satellite groups. With the coming of the successor Council, LCUSA, many of these informal associations were readily brought into the central agency itself. In this fashion a movement slowly but steadily created effective structures for itself.

Slow but Steady Progress

Progress was slow. There were setbacks and failures and opportunities missed. Uncertainties about doctrinal unity, separate ethnic traditions, differing procedural patterns, personality clashes, competitions among national bodies—these factors and others defeated or slowed up many proposals for common action. In the wake of NLC pioneering in public relations the national bodies developed their separate and often high-powered publicity and public relations programs. Repeatedly, even after welfare was a recognized area of NLC activity, particular welfare projects failed to receive cooperative support because of the organizational problems of securing budgetary support from several out-of-phase national organizations. In the 1950's the executive director reported that more cooperative opportunities were rejected than accepted, primarily because the NLC was not supposed to relate directly to congregations but only to national bodies. In the 1960's the Council's executives were asked whether the NLC reached its potential in their particular fields. A number of them were able to point out important work that had not been undertaken. The Council was not only the living symbol of a will to unity; it was at the same time a concrete symbol of the tensions within American Lutheranism and an ever-present evidence of the limited nature of Lutheran unity.

But, measured by decades, progress was steady and the resulting structures were quite effective within the limitations of the Council's mandate. Previous chapters have traced the NLC's growth in periods of seven and fourteen years. After an initial seven-year period in which dramatic overseas responsibilities got the young organization off to a good start, there followed fourteen lean years in which the heartbeat of the organization—public relations—remained steady despite inadequate nurture. Then, for fourteen years during and following World War II, rapid and enthusiastic expansion of services marked the golden age of the Council's life. During the final fourteen years of the Council's existence its services settled into more of a routine, though there was marked growth in the volume and effectiveness of much that was undertaken. One could either say that emergency operations subsided or claim that emergencies became the routine of the organization's tasks. In the latter half of this phase the NLC's programs altered subtly in facing a changing age and in preparation for its own metamorphosis into new forms in 1967. Looking at the whole span of years it is fair to say that progress in cooperation was steady and that the Council's programs were impressively effective.

Unity, Identity, Mission

How does one assess the impact of the National Lutheran Council and its flowing stream of cooperative services in behalf of America's Lutherans? It can be summarized under the headings of unity, identity, and mission. The most obvious impact is in the area of Christian unity. The evidence is overwhelming that Lutherans who worked together across all boundaries learned to trust one another as fellow Lutherans and friends. This has been repeatedly asserted as the personal experience of the participants. And the record of accomplishments could not have been achieved had it been otherwise. Doctrinal discussions may be essential to Lutheran union, but they can easily produce disagreement and rancor unless there is goodwill and mutual trust at the outset; the process of planning and carrying out cooperative activities did in fact build such a platform of mutual trust. The NLC and its satellite organizations have made a tremendous contribution in nurturing Lutheran unity and in moving American Lutherans toward larger organizational union, simply by bringing diverse people together in the doing of common tasks. And Americans through this agency have been leaders in building an international Lutheran fellowship as well.

It should also be noted that cooperative Lutheranism made a sizeable contribution to the larger ecumenical movement. In fact, the Lutheran movement was an integral part of this larger twentieth century trend. In many subtle ways participation in Lutheran cooperation raised men's sights to the larger Christian community. Quite a few of the NLC's programs—particularly in emergency relief, representations before the government, chaplaincy services—brought direct involvement with the programs and personnel of other churches. Occasionally it worked the other way, so that preoccupation with Lutheran cooperation limited what some Lutherans would have contributed to interdenominational activities. But for most Lutherans most of the time the NLC served to move them closer to other ecumenical endeavors. Experience with people who were not too different (other Lutherans) prepared the way for fruitful contacts with those who seemed more strange or distant. The life of the National Lutheran

Council has been a useful introduction into wider conciliar experience for hosts of people. Incidentally, a number of NLC executives have moved on into comparable posts in the National Council of Churches, the Lutheran World Federation, and the World Council of Churches, providing able leadership for these broader organizations.

A second major impact of the National Lutheran Council points in the direction of a new image, self-identity and destiny for America's Lutherans. Here the Council was not so much the embodiment of a movement as it was a focus for major trends in the history of American Lutheranism itself. As one church leader put it: "The involvement of most United States Lutheran Churches in the competitive forces of today's world comes to dramatic focus in the work of the NLC."

Concerned for correct understanding of the Gospel and proud of their theology, Lutherans knew that true faith is active in love and expresses itself readily in outgoing good works. But American Lutheran immigrants had had no strong record of social concern beyond some worthy welfare efforts which largely served their own people. In the twentieth century this has been changing to a remarkable degree. Coupled with a rediscovery of Luther's theology and the social ethic inherent in it, this new and broader interest in social action is a major trend in the story of American Lutheranism. The NLC played a major role in it. Pouring resources into overseas relief and rehabilitation, aiding refugees and influencing immigrant legislation, studies by social trends committees, a rural life and an urban church program— these were expressions of that concern; just as often, these were prophetic stimulators of that concern, especially as effective publicity interpreted such programs to Lutherans and the nation.

A more speculative conclusion would be that such programs actually stimulated the theological renaissance that accompanied them, encouraging theologians to rediscover the social dimensions of the Gospel from a Lutheran perspective. It is clear, at any rate, that in the modern world theologizing becomes more exciting as it comes to grips with the issues of contemporary society. And the NLC was one major agency through which American Lutherans wrestled with contemporary and pressing social needs.

In fact, the way in which Lutherans responded together in meeting the crises of special needs after World War I and, to a heightened degree, during and after World War II, was the largest single factor in changing the image of American Lutheranism. Scattered immigrant enclaves started to see themselves as giving churches, able to return help to their mother countries, a force to be reckoned with on the American scene. And over the decades other Americans and Christians around the world have become newly aware that American Lutherans were lively in their interests, capable of generosity, and possessed of considerable potential. The activities of the NLC, including its effective public relations work, helped to nurture and to focus this new self-confidence and more positive public image.

Somewhat more conjectural is the conclusion that the National Lutheran Council, as it has funneled Lutheran services out to the general society and around the world, has held up before a newly-matured and newly-influential American Lutheranism the image of a prophetic and servant church as its destined role within the larger American and ecumenical scene. Certainly LWA and LWR programs have taken the lead in helping American Lutherans to interpret their responsibilities more broadly. In the early decades of the century the church's outreach was interpreted largely as evangelism and conversions into the Lutheran church, on the one hand, and as acts of relief and mercy for fellow Lutherans, on the other hand. During the 1950's and the 1960's the NLC was representing Lutherans in the search for a public consensus on national issues, in resettling Tanzanian animists, in providing vocational training for Arab Moslems, in entering friendly dialogue with the Roman Catholic Church. In our day, when Christians take seriously their mandate to serve the world they find themselves acting in cooperation.

This brings us to the third aspect of the Council's impact: It has provided the cutting edge of mission as American Lutherans have expressed their sense of mission. Not that the NLC has carried out the main missionary activities of the cooperating bodies. For the most part it has not been directly operational but has simply coordinated and channeled the activities of other church agencies. But most of the exciting new work has had to be done in concert to be fully effective. On the cutting edge of mission, in shaping new thrusts, American Lutherans have found cooperation to be essential. For just this reason the Council and its companion organizations have often attracted pioneering leadership for the sparking of their programs. For this reason the top executives of the various church bodies have been willing to spend many days each year in the planning and policy sessions of the Council and its committees. Not only were they building mutual trust as a basis for substantial Lutheran unity; they were bending their energies in a common effort to further Christ's mission.

The movement which the NLC embodied was not only saying: We want to do things *together*. It was also saying: We want *to do things* together. Not only was the movement part of a larger ecumenical movement; it was also *an essential expression of the life of the church*. Without this movement and its institutional organs Lutherans in America would have been seriously crippled in fulfilling their mission to the modern world. Their efforts would have been truncated, sporadic, and much less effective.

The Conciliar Movement

When one ponders the significance of the National Lutheran Council one finds himself pondering the meaning of the whole modern conciliar movement.

With the coming of the denominational pattern of church life in recent centuries, with its acceptance of separate church organizations overlapping one another in areas of responsibility, councils of churches became a necessity for expressing Christian unity and witness. Whoso says denominations, implies also councils. And it is an obvious historical fact that the conciliar movement has been powerful in the twentieth century. In attempting to evidence the marks of the church—especially the unity and the apostolic witness—denominations have had to rely on councils of churches. In seeking to express the full-orbed Body of Christ, church bodies have had to depend on councils of churches.

Herein lies the ecclesiological significance of councils of churches.

American Lutherans have been reluctant to participate fully in the conciliar movement. Many of them have learned the value of the conciliar experience through the National Lutheran Council. They have been helped to a more complete expression of the church's life.

It is entirely correct to say that the National Lutheran Council was simply the agency of the participating church bodies through which they carried out some of their functions. It is equally correct to say that the National Lutheran Council, and the movement for unity and mission which it embodied, provided American Lutherans with a fuller manifestation of the church's essential nature.

Notes

CHAPTER I

Prelude and Beginnings

1. Letter from Lauritz Larsen to Adolph Hult, March 26, 1919. All letters and documents referred to in the notes of this book — unless otherwise specified—are located in original or copy in the archives of the NLC, "The Archives of Cooperative Lutheranism," located at L.C. U.S.A. headquarters in New York City.

2. More detail and documentation on this and other events immediately preceding the birth of the NLC are given in the author's "Beginnings of the National Lutheran Council" in *Concordia Historical Institute Quarterly*, October 1967.

3. This sequence of events preceding the Harrisburg meeting is constructed from letters and materials in the NLC archival file on its beginnings, including an undated copy of the invitation quoted following. See also the reference in note two above.

4. Doubt is cast upon the constructive value of his efforts by a letter from Lauritz Larsen to Pannkoke, June 25, 1918, in which Larsen states that efforts to call a meeting in the name of the Lutheran Bureau are not helpful and have created resentment on the part of "at least one influential president."

5. The official minutes simply stated that fifteen were present and reported the three resolutions adopted. In the NLC archives is a typed copy of a more complete record kept by the appointed secretary, O. H. Pannkoke, from which the present description is drawn.

6. As listed in the minutes they were:

(1) General Synod: Dr. V. G. A. Tressler, Dr. John Seibert, Mr. Charles J. Driever, Mr. C. H. Boyer, the Honorable John Zimmerman, Dr. H. L. Yarger, Dr. F. H. Knubel; (2) General Council: Dr. T. E. Schmauk, Dr. W. D. C. Keiter, Dr. Charles M. Jacobs, the Reverend G. K. Rubrecht, Dr. H. A. Weller, Dr. E. F. Krauss, Dr. J. Stump; (3) Joint Synod of Ohio: Dr. C. H. L. Schuette, the Reverend M. P. G. Doermann; (4) Synod of Iowa and Other States: Dr. F. Richter, Dr. M. Fritschel; (5) Augustana Synod: Dr. G. A. Brandelle, Mr. N. A. Nelson, the Reverend P. Peterson, Mr. C. J. Appell; (6) Norwegian Lutheran Church: Dr. H. G. Stub, Mr. H. S. Holstad, Professor L. W. Boe, the Reverend J. A. O. Stub; (7) Norwegian Lutheran Free Church: the Reverend John Mattson, Dr. George Sverdrup; (8) Danish Lutheran Church: Mr. H. P. Rasmussen; (9) National Lutheran Commission: Secretary Lauritz Larsen.

CHAPTER II

Establishing Domestic Patterns (1918-1925)

1. *Minutes,* Joint Committee on Doctrine and Practice, NLC, March 11, 1919, pp. 10-12.

2. See *Lutheran Church Review,* XXXVIII (April, 1919), pp. 187-212.

3. *Minutes,* Joint Conference on Doctrine and Practice, NLC, January, 1920, p. 19.

4. For details on this development see E. Clifford Nelson in *The Lutheran Church Among Norwegian-Americans,* II (Minneapolis: Augsburg Publishing House, 1960), pp. 298-99.

5. *Ibid.,* p. 289.

6. The following discussion of these two schools is informed by Nelson's account, *ibid.,* pp. 283 ff.

7. Quoted in *Minutes,* NLC, April 4, 1922, p. 22.

8. *Minutes,* Executive Committee, NLC, December 7, 1921, p. 8.

9. Letter to NLC, November 28, 1921.

10. Letter to pastors from S. J. McDowell of Baltimore in 1923.

11. See NLC archival file on the death of Larsen.

12. Larsen's trip to Europe and Transylvania in 1920 is recorded in a lengthy diary.

CHAPTER III

A Dramatic Overseas Role (1918-1925)

1. *Minutes,* NLC, May 3, 1921, p. 21.

2. These contacts have been described with more detail and documentation in the author's "American Lutheran Contacts with their Romanian Brethren in the 1920's" in *Geschichtswirklichkeit und Glaubensbewährung, Festschrift für Bischof Friedrich Müller,* Franklin Clark Fry, ed. (Stuttgart: Evangelisches Verlagswerk, 1967), pp. 245-253.

3. *Minutes,* European Commission, NLC, October 7, 1919, p. 9.

4. *Annual Report,* NLC, November 6, 1919, Supplement, p. 60.

5. See *Minutes,* NLC, December 18, 1919, p. 8.

6. *Minutes,* NLC, December 11, 1918, p. 3.

7. *Minutes,* NLC, May 3, 1921, p. 25.

8. *Proceedings,* NLC, 1923, pp. 56, 60.

9. See *The Lutheran World Almanac for 1926* (New York: National Lutheran Council, 1925), p. 27.

10. For an informal portrait see Samuel Trexler, *John A. Morehead: A Biography* (New York: G. P. Putnam's Sons, 1938). The Hoover quotation is found on page 149.

11. Letter, September 24, 1919.

12. Annual Report, NLC, November 3, 1921, pp. 62-63.

CHAPTER IV

Through Thick and Thin Together (1926-1938)

1. After Eisenach (1923) members of this committee were: J. A. Morehead, chairman; L. W. Boe (President of St. Olaf College), Northfield, Minnesota; Ludwig Ihmels, Dresden, Germany; Wilhelm F. von Pechmann, Munich, Germany; Alfred Th. Jørgensen, Copenhagen, Denmark; Per Pehrsson, Göteborg, Sweden.

2. *Lutheran,* April 1, 1926, p. 4.

3. *Minutes,* Annual Meeting, 1931, p. 15.

4. Letter, J. A. Morehead to L. W. Boe, September 11, 1925.

5. At times during the first decade of the Council Mees served faithfully as a substitute at the executive's desk in New York and as a European Commissioner.

6. *Minutes,* Annual Meeting, 1932, p. 43.

7. *Minutes,* Annual Meeting, 1926, p. 9.

8. *Minutes,* Annual Meeting, 1934, p. 47.

9. *Minutes,* Annual Meeting, 1926, p. 7.

10. The story of the establishment of the American Lutheran Conference is told in Fred W. Meuser, *The Formation of The American Lutheran Church* (Columbus, Ohio: The Wartburg Press, 1958), pp. 235 ff. See also Nelson, *The Lutheran Church Among Norwegian-Americans,* II, pp. 303 ff.

11. Evidence of this defensive stance and evaluation of it is given in Meuser, *ibid.,* and in Nelson, *ibid.*

CHAPTER V

The Decisive Years (1930-1938)

1. *Minutes,* Annual Meeting, 1937, p. 80.

2. *Ibid.*

3. *Minutes,* Annual Meeting, 1933, p. 36.

4. *Ibid.,* p. 23.

5. *Minutes,* Annual Meeting, 1934, pp. 12-13.

6. *Minutes,* Annual Meeting, 1932, p. 27.

7. *Minutes,* Annual Meeting, 1933, p. 34.

8. In a letter to J. A. Aasgaard, October 29, 1942, quoted in Nelson, *op. cit.,* p. 302, n. 51.

9. *Minutes,* Annual Meeting, 1935, p. 9.

10. *Minutes,* Annual Meeting, 1932, p. 8.

11. *Minutes,* Annual Meeting, 1937, p. 78.

CHAPTER VI

A Ready and Rousing Response (1939-1945)

1. *Agenda,* Annual Meeting, 1941, "Report of the Department of Welfare."

2. *Agenda,* Annual Meeting, 1940, "Report of the Department of Welfare."

3. *Agenda,* Annual Meeting, 1944, p. 69.

4. This phrase, used by O. H. Pannkoke (*A Great Church Finds Itself*, published by the author in Quitman, Georgia, in 1966) to characterize a discovery during the World War I period (see p. 94), is doubly apt for the changed atmosphere among Lutherans in the World War II period.

5. *Agenda*, Annual Meeting, 1944, p. 82.

6. *Agenda*, Annual Meeting, 1946, p. 51.

7. This point is made by the Reverend Rollin G. Shaffer, since 1948 the promotional secretary and later assistant director of LWA, in his 15-page history called "LWA, A Quarter Century of Christian Compassion," published in the December 1965 and January 1966 numbers of the *National Lutheran*.

8. An outline narrative and the pertinent documents on this subject are found in Richard C. Wolf, *Documents of Lutheran Unity in America* (Philadelphia: Fortress Press, 1966), pp. 466 ff.

9. *Minutes*, Annual Meeting, 1942, p. 8.

10. *Agenda*, Annual Meeting, 1943, p. 26.

11. Osborne Hauge, *Lutherans Working Together: A History of the National Lutheran Council, 1918-1943* (New York: National Lutheran Council, 1945), with a supplementary chapter by Ralph H. Long on the years 1943-1945.

12. First headquarters for the NLC had been in the Knabe Building at 39th St. and Fifth Avenue, New York. In 1927 the Council moved to ULCA headquarters at 39 E. 35th St., and in 1944 accompanied that body to headquarters in the former Morgan mansion on Madison Ave. In 1950 the NLC took up separate quarters at 50 Madison Ave. on Madison Square for its remaining years.

13. *Agenda*, Annual Meeting, 1943, p. 30.

14. *Agenda*, Annual Meeting, 1959, p. 85.

15. Long's chapter in Hauge, *Lutherans Working Together*, p. 114.

CHAPTER VII

Postward Crescendo (1946-1952)

1. *Minutes*, Annual Meeting, February, 1948, pp. 15-16.

2. See Wolf, *Documents in Lutheran Unity*, pp. 472 ff., and Abdel Ross Wentz, *A Basic History of Lutheranism in America*, revised edition (Philadelphia: Fortress Press, 1964), pp. 349 ff.

3. The four are listed separately in an early form of Long's report to the 1945 annual meeting. For the fifth, see *Minutes*, Annual Meeting, p. 21.

4. See the 32-page booklet by A. Henry Hetland, *Ferment* (Chicago: National Lutheran Council, 1966), for an impressionistic description of this aspect of NLC work, written by the last of its executive secretaries.

5. *Uniform Report 1950*, NLC, pp. 9-10.

6. Richard W. Solberg in *As Between Brothers* (Minneapolis: Augsburg Publishing House, 1957) has told this story in greater detail from the perspective of world Lutheranism and the Department of World Service of the Lutheran World Federation.

7. *Agenda*, Annual Meeting, 1945, pp. 27-28.

8. *Agenda*, Annual Meeting, 1945, p. 53.

9. *Minutes*, Annual Meeting, 1946, p. 23.

10. *Minutes*, Annual Meeting, 1947, p. 25.

11. Solberg's account in *As Between Brothers* features Michelfelder's experiences and accomplishments.

12. *Minutes*, Annual Meeting, 1946, p. 30.

13. Quoted from Solberg, *op. cit.*, p. 43.

CHAPTER VIII

Broad Streams of Steady Traffic (1953-1966)

1. *Agenda*, Annual Meeting, 1956, p. 232.

2. *Agenda*, Annual Meeting, 1961, p. 6 of "Division of American Missions, Annual Report, 1960."

3. Letter to his secretary, received February 16, 1967.

4. *Minutes*, Lutheran Film Associates, September 28, 1966, p. 6.

5. *Agenda*, Annual Meeting, 1964, pp. 40-41.

6. Letter to Donald R. Heiges, February 1, 1966.

CHAPTER IX

The Changing Landscape (1959-1966)

1. *Agenda*, Annual Meeting, 1958, pp. 71-73.

2. *Uniform Report 1965*, NLC, p. 2.

3. *Agenda*, Annual Meeting, 1966, p. 189.

4. *Agenda*, Annual Meeting, 1966, p. 45.

Bibliography

Main sources for this study have been the minutes and the archives of the National Lutheran Council. This latter depository, now a part of the archives of the Lutheran Council in the United States of America, is rightly called "Archives of Cooperative Lutheranism," since it is much broader than the NLC records and correspondence, including archival materials of most of the cooperative organizations of twentieth-century American Lutheranism, as well as the Lutheran World Convention.

These archives include 1,100 archive boxes of NLC correspondence and documents (a conservative estimate of 1,100,000 manuscript items), together with an additional 400 boxes (400,000 manuscript items) of affiliated and related agencies. In addition, the collection contains all news releases from 1918 to 1966 and all publications of the Council.

The Minutes and Reports of the Council have been produced in the following ways:

1919–1921 ... Annual reports were printed and paper bound. These did not include minutes of the annual meeting. Apparently these printed reports were distributed to seminary libraries.

1918–1936 ... Annual Reports and Minutes included as one, with title "Annual Meeting," mimeographed. Separate mimeographed Minutes of special and other meetings of the Council.

1937–1966 ... "Annual Meeting" mimeographed in two separate sections with separate paging for Reports and for Minutes.

1918–1966 . . . Minutes of Committees, Divisions, Commissions, Bureaus as their meetings occurred. Mimeographed.

In addition to the above Reports and Minutes, a Uniform Report was issued annually for 1947 through 1953, and biennially for 1954-1965.

Secondary works with overall descriptions of the Council's history include:

Osborne Hauge, *Lutherans Working Together* (New York: National Lutheran Council, 1945).

Helen Knubel, "National Lutheran Council," in *The Encyclopedia of the Lutheran Church* (Minneapolis: Augsburg Publishing House, 1965).

Abdel Ross Wentz, *A Basic History of Lutheranism in America* (Philadelphia: Fortress Press, 1964).

Other secondary works with material directly relevant to Council history (as cited in the footnotes) include:

Lutheran World Almanac (New York: National Lutheran Council, various editions in 1920's and 1930's).

Fred W. Meuser, *The Formation of the American Lutheran Church* (Columbus, Ohio: Wartburg Press, 1958).

E. Clifford Nelson and Eugene L. Fevold, *The Lutheran Church among Norwegian-Americans* (Minneapolis: Augsburg Publishing House, 1960).

O. H. Pannkoke, *A Great Church Finds Itself* (Quitman, Georgia: by the author, 1966).

Richard W. Solberg, *As Between Brothers* (Minneapolis: Augsburg Publishing House, 1957).

Samuel Trexler, *John A. Morehead: A Biography* (New York: G. P. Putnam's Sons, 1938).

Richard C. Wolf, *Documents of Lutheran Unity in America* (Philadelphia: Fortress Press, 1966).

Officers and Councillors

(In earlier years called Representatives or Commissioners)

Presidents

Dr. H. G. Stub	1918-1920
Dr. Lauritz Larsen	1921-1923
Dr. C. H. L. Schuette	1923-1924
Dr. G. A. Brandelle	1925-1932
Dr. C. C. Hein	1933-1936
Dr. Ellis B. Burgess	1937-1940
Dr. P. O. Bersell	1941-1944
Dr. Rees Edgar Tulloss	1945-1947
Dr. Wm. G. Sodt	1948-1949
Dr. Lawrence Stavig	1950-1952
Dr. Oscar A. Benson	1953-1955
Dr. F. Eppling Reinartz	1956-1958
Dr. Norman A. Menter	1959-1961
Dr. Raymond M. Olson	1962-1964
Dr. George F. Harkins	1965-1966

Vice Presidents

The Hon. John L. Zimmerman	1918
Dr. F. H. Knubel	1919-1920
Dr. C. H. L. Schuette	1921-1923
Dr. G. A. Brandelle	1923-1924
Dr. C. C. Hein	1925-1932
Dr. N. C. Carlsen	1933-1936
Dr. T. O. Burntvedt	1937-1940
Dr. Martin Anderson	1941-1944
Dr. Wm. G. Sodt	1945-1947
Dr. Martin Anderson	1948-1949

201

Dr. Oscar A. Benson	1950-1952
Dr. Henry F. Schuh	1953-1955
Dr. Norman A. Menter	1956-1958
Dr. Raymond M. Olson	1959-1961
Dr. George F. Harkins	1962-1964
Dr. William Larsen	1965-1966

Secretaries

Dr. Lauritz Larsen	1918-1919
Dr. Peter Peterson	1920-1924
Dr. J. A. O. Stub	1925-1926
Dr. N. C. Carlsen	1927-1932
Dr. M. R. Hamsher	1933-1936
Dr. Peter Peterson	1937-1940
Dr. Armin G. Weng	1941-1944
Dr. Martin Anderson	1945-1947
Dr. Armin G. Weng	1948-1950
Dr. Rees Edgar Tulloss	1951-1953
Dr. F. Eppling Reinartz	1954-1955
Dr. Raymond M. Olson	1956-1958
Mr. Harold LeVander	1959-1961
Mr. Cyrus Rachie	1962-1964
The Hon. Hilbert Schauer	1965-1966

Treasurers

The Hon. E. F. Eilert	1919-1940
Mr. S. F. Telleen	1941-1951
Mr. Fred C. Eggerstedt	1952-1963
Dr. Roy L. Reierson	1964-1966

Councillors (*Present at organizational meeting, 1918)

Dr. J. A. Aasgaard	1926-1955	Ex. Com. 1931-1936, 1941, 1944-1954
Dr. Martin Anderson	1941-1956	Ex. Com. 1941-1949
The Rev. M. N. Andreason	1922-1925	Ex. Com. 1922-1925
*Mr. C. J. Appel	1918	
Mrs. C. W. Baker, Jr.	1949-1950, 1953-1956	
Dr. Henry H. Bagger	1951-1956	Ex. Com. 1951
Mr. Charles L. Balcer	1966	
Dr. G. H. Bechtold	1939-1956	
Dr. Alfred L. Beck	1959-1962	
Dr. Oscar A. Benson	1945-1959	Ex. Com. 1950-1959
The Rev. Leopold W. Bernhard	1963-1966	
Dr. P. O. Bersell	1936-1954	Ex. Com. 1936, 1941-1954
Mr. A. J. Bjork	1956	

Mr. Carl E. Bock	1963-1966		
Dr. Julius Bodensieck	1943-1946, 1949-1950		
*Dr. L. W. Boe	1918,	Ex. Com.	1927-1930
	1924-1942		1937-1942
The Rev. Wynne C. Boliek	1959-1961		
*Mr. C. H. Boyer	1918		
Mr. Bart Brammer	1959		
*Dr. G. A. Brandelle	1918-1935	Ex. Com. 1918-1935	
Dr. John R. Brokhoff	1952-1956		
Dr. P. D. Brown	1939-1948	Ex. Com. 1942-1944	
Mr. Dale Bruning	1959-1960		
Mr. Gordon Bubolz	1948		
Dr. Ellis B. Burgess	1931-1941	Ex. Com. 1931-1940	
Mr. Milton V. Burgess	1957-1962		
The Rev. Lloyd L. Burke	1963-1966		
The Rev. Lyle C. Burns	1949-1951		
Dr. T. O. Burntvedt	1931-1958	Ex. Com. 1931-1958	
Dr. N. C. Carlsen	1926-1950	Ex. Com. 1927-1950	
Mr. Thomas Casto	1965-1966		
Dr. Voigt R. Cromer	1949-1955		
The Rev. Paul M. de Freese	1963-1964		
Dr. Paul W. Dieckman	1965-1966		
*The Rev. M. P. G. Doermann	1918-1922, 1934-1938		
Dr. A. T. Dorf	1937-1942	Ex. Com. 1937-1940	
*Mr. Charles J. Driever	1918		
Dr. S. C. Eastvold	1956-1960		
Dr. Frank K. Efird	1956-1962	Ex. Com. 1959-1962	
Mr. Fred C. Eggerstedt	1955-1958	Ex. Com. 1955-1958	
The Hon. E. F. Eilert	1919-1943	Ex. Com. 1919-1940	
The Rev. Oscar E. Engebretson	1956-1966		
Dr. August Engelbrecht	1951-1954	Ex. Com. 1952-1954	
Mr. Herbert Engelbrecht	1953-1960		
Dr. A. H. Ewald	1961-1966		
Dr. A. Ejnar Farstrup	1961-1962	Ex. Com. 1961-1962	
Dr. Charles B. Foelsch	1951-1958		
Dr. George W. Forell	1963-1966		
The Rev. H. L. Foss	1957-1960		
Dr. C. A. Freed	1920-1938		
*Dr. M. Fritschel	1918		
Dr. Franklin C. Fry	1945-1966	Ex. Com. 1946-1966	
The Rev. I. Gertsen	1919-1921	Ex. Com. 1919-1921	
The Rev. P. Gotke	1919-1925	Ex. Com. 1924-1925	
Dr. W. H. Greever	1945-1948		
Mr. G. F. Greiner	1920-1946		
Dr. T. F. Gullixson	1941-1955		
The Rev. E. E. Gynild	1924		
Dr. A. Haapanen	1942-1950	Ex. Com. 1943-1950	
Dr. J. A. W. Haas	1927-1932, 1935-1937		
Mr. Walter R. Hagey	1963-1966		
Dr. M. R. Hamsher	1933-1948	Ex. Com. 1935-1936,	
		1947	

Dr. George F. Harkins	1961-1966	Ex. Com. 1962-1966
Dr. R. E. Haugan	1945-1955, 1961-1964	
Mr. Eugene S. Heckathorn	1959-1962	
Mr. Harold Hegstrom	1944-1952	
Dr. Donald R. Heiges	1959-1960	Ex. Com. 1959-1962
Mr. George A. Heimrich	1954	
Dr. C. C. Hein	1923-1936	Ex. Com. 1925-1936
Judge James F. Henninger	1953-1958	Ex. Com. 1954
Dr. Bernhard Hillila	1963-1966	Ex. Com. 1963-1966
Dr. C. S. B. Hoel	1931	
The Rev. K. A. Hoessel	1919-1925	
*Mr. H. S. Holstad	1918	
Mrs. Ruth G. Horting	1957-1962	
*Dr. Charles M. Jacobs	1918-1931	Ex. Com. 1922-1930
Mr. Arthur H. Jacobson	1961-1966	
Dr. Alfred Jensen	1943-1961	Ex. Com. 1945-1960
Dr. Erling N. Jensen	1963-1966	Ex. Com. 1963-1966
The Rev. Hans C. Jersild	1951-1956	Ex. Com. 1951-1956
The Rev. B. B. Jonsson	1919-1920	
*Dr. W. D. C. Keiter	1918	
Dr. Holger F. Kilander	1953-1961	
*Dr. F. H. Knubel	1918-1922, 1941-1944	Ex. Com. 1918-1919, 1941
Dr. Edwin H. Knudten	1963-1964	
Dr. P. W. Koller	1925-1937	
*Dr. E. F. Krauss	1918	
Dr. C. E. Krumbholz	1932-1939	
*Dr. Lauritz Larsen	1918-1923	Ex. Com. 1918-1923
Dr. William Larsen	1957-1966	Ex. Com. 1957-1966
Dr. Robert E. Lee	1957-1962	
Dr. Gerhard E. Lenski	1949-1950	
Mr. Harold LeVander	1955-1966	Ex. Com. 1959-1966
Dr. Paul Lindberg	1963-1966	
Mr. Erwin H. List	1955-1962	Ex. Com. 1958-1961
Mr. Howard Logan	1960	
Dr. Malvin H. Lundeen	1955-1966	Ex. Com. 1955-1966
The Hon. Harold R. Lundgren	1941-1943	
*The Rev. John Mattson	1918	
Dr. Norman A. Menter	1955-1966	Ex. Com. 1955-1966
Dr. R. W. Miottel	1955-1958	
Dr. Paul Moeller	1963-1966	
*Mr. N. A. Nelson	1918	
Mr. Joseph G. Norby	1951-1954	
Dr. Joshua Oden	1941	
The Rev. K. K. Olafson	1924-1930, 1938-1940	
Mr. Karl J. Olson	1936-1940	
Dr. O. N. Olson	1942-1944	
Dr. Raymond M. Olson	1956-1966	Ex. Com. 1956-1964
Dr. Harold C. Osterman	1953-1956	
The Rev. Floyd A. Paules	1965-1966	

*Dr. Peter Peterson	1918-1940	Ex. Com. 1920-1924, 1937-1940
Dr. E. P. Pfatteicher	1931-1943	Ex. Com. 1937-1940
The Rev. E. Poppen	1926-1950	Ex. Com. 1926-1930, 1937-1941, 1947-1950
Dr. Kenneth Priebe	1965	
Dr. Dwight F. Putnam	1949-1950	
The Rev. J. N. Quello	1961-1966	
Mr. Cyrus Rachie	1959-1966	Ex. Com. 1962-1966
*Mr. H. P. Rasmussen	1918	
Dr. Harold Rasmussen	1963-1966	
The Rev. E. H. Rausch	1931-1938	Ex. Com. 1931-1936
Dr. F. Eppling Reinartz	1947-1962	Ex. Com. 1951-1962
Mrs. M. F. Rheingaus	1955-1958	
Mr. Robert R. Rhyne	1963-1966	
*Dr. F. Richter	1918-1919	Ex. Com. 1918-1919
Dr. A. N. Rogness	1956-1966	
*The Rev. G. K. Rubrecht	1918	
Dr. W. C. Schaeffer, Jr.	1947-1950	
The Hon. Hilbert Schauer	1961-1966	
Dr. J. J. Scherer	1944-1948	
Dr. M. G. G. Scherer	1923-1931	Ex. Com. 1926-1931
Dr. Fredrik A. Schiotz	1955-1966	Ex. Com. 1955-1966
*Dr. T. E. Schmauk	1918-1919	
Dr. Henry F. Schock	1951-1952	
*Dr. C. H. L. Schuette	1918-1925, 1937-1940	Ex. Com. 1918-1924
Dr. Henry F. Schuh	1938-1942, 1951-1962	Ex. Com. 1951-1961
The Rev. T. J. C. Schuldt	1952-1954	
Dr. George Schultz	1961-1966	
Mrs. John Paul Shannon	1959-1962	
*Dr. John Seibert	1918	
Dr. Herman W. Siefkes	1947-1948, 1957-1960	
The Rev. O. H. Sletten	1919-1921	
Dr. Charles J. Smith	1920-1928	
Mrs. G. Morris Smith (Mrs. Ruth Juram)	1951, 1963-1966	
Dr. Wm. G. Sodt	1939-1952	Ex. Com. 1942-1951
Dr. R. C. Sorrick	1944-1945	
Dr. Lawrence Stavig	1947-1955, 1950-1954	
Dr. Lloyd W. Steckel	1929-1938	
Mr. E. B. Steensland	1918-1923	
Dr. John M. Stensvaag	1959-1966	Ex. Com. 1959-1966
*Dr. H. G. Stub	1918-1925	Ex. Com. 1918-1925
*Dr. J. A. O. Stub	1918, 1924-1940	Ex. Com. 1925-1926
*Dr. J. Stump	1918	
*Dr. George Sverdrup	1918	
Dr. L. Ralph Tabor	1953-1958	Ex. Com. 1956-1958
Mr. S. F. Telleen	1941-1954	Ex. Com. 1941-1953
The Rev. Christian J. Thearle	1965-1966	

The Rev. N. S. Thorlaksson	1921	
The Rev. Raymond Tiemeyer	1963-1964	
Dr. Rees Edgar Tulloss	1938-1958	Ex. Com. 1945-1958
Dr. A. J. Traver	1947-1952	
*Dr. V. G. A. Tressler	1918-1923	
Dr. Levering Tyson	1947-1948	
The Rev. H. J. Urdahl	1925-1930	Ex. Com. 1926-1930
The Rev. Herbert W. Veler	1959-1962	
Dr. H. Torry Walker	1946	
Dr. John Wargelin	1951-1955	Ex. Com. 1951-1954
Dr. Raymond Wargelin	1956-1962	Ex. Com. 1956-1962
*Dr. H. A. Weller	1918-1925	Ex. Com. 1918-1925
Dr. Armin G. Weng	1938-1952	Ex. Com. 1941-1944, 1948-1950
Dr. Abdel Ross Wentz	1948-1954	Ex. Com. 1948-1954
Dr. Paul L. Wetzler	1947-1958	
The Rev. John Whetstone	1955-1956	
Mr. Andrew J. White, Jr.	1957-1962	
Dr. Robbin B. Wolf	1944-1946	
Dr. Raymond Wood	1963-1964	
*Dr. H. L. Yarger	1918	
The Rev. Harold Yochum	1941-1960	
Dr. Wm. L. Young	1951-1962	
Dr. Royall A. Yount	1965-1966	
*Mr. John L. Zimmerman	1918-1919	
Dr. A. A. Zinck	1939-1946	

STAFF

Elected or appointed by Executive Committee

ADMINISTRATION

Executive Director (General Secretary, Executive Secretary)

Dr. Lauritz Larsen	1918-1923
Dr. Oscar Mees	1923
Dr. John A. Morehead	1923-1930
Dr. F. H. Meyer	1930
Dr. Ralph H. Long	1930-1948
Dr. Paul C. Empie	1948-1966

Assistant Executive Director (Administrative Assistant, Assistant to Executive Director)

Dr. Paul C. Empie	1944-1948
Dr. Carl E. Lund-Quist	1949-1950
Dr. Charles Carroll	1953-1956
Dr. J. Robert Busche	1956-1966

Assistant Treasurer

Mrs. Mildred Meyer	1942-1949
Mrs. Marguerite Feder	1948-1966
Mr. Sanfrid Ruohoniemi (Comptroller)	1950-1956

LUTHERAN WORLD ACTION

Director
Dr. Paul C. Empie   1944-1966

Assistant Director
The Rev. Rollin Shaffer   1950-1966

Production Manager
Mr. Harold Skelton   1956-1966

PUBLIC RELATIONS

(not so designated until 1945, when Division of PR was organized)

Executive Secretary
Dr. Carl E. Lund-Quist   1946-1950
Dr. Joseph Simonson   1951-1953
Dr. Harold E. Hammond   1956-1957
Dr. Philip A. Johnson   1958-1966

Public Information (Lutheran Bureau, News Bureau)
Secretary
Dr. O. H. Pannkoke   1919-1920
Dr. Howard R. Gold   1921-1923
Mr. W. P. Elson   1924-1933, 1943-1945
Dr. C. K. Fegley   1933-1937
Mr. Osborne Hauge   1937-1943
Mr. Louis Schenk   1946-1947
Dr. Erik Modean   1948-1966

Research & Statistics (Library)
Secretary
Dr. George Linn Kieffer   1919-1937
Miss Mary Boozer   1938-1944
Miss Marjorie Teisberg   1946-1948
Miss Ruth Curby   1949-1953
Miss Helen M. Knubel   1954-1966

Washington Office
Secretary
Dr. Robert E. Van Deusen   1949-1966

Radio & TV
Secretary
Mr. Rolf Hertsgaard   1956-1957
Miss Betty Barth   1958-1963

Publications
Secretary
Mr. Alex Liepa   1956-1962
The Rev. Glenn C. Stone   1962-1966

WELFARE

(Department 1940-1945; Division 1946-1966)

Executive Secretary

Dr. Clarence E. Krumbholz	1940-1954
Dr. Henry J. Whiting	1955-1962
The Rev. G. S. Thompson	1963-1966

Consultants

Miss Henriette Lund	1944-1948, 1950-1955
Dr. Carl R. Plack	1945-1966
Dr. Henry J. Whiting	1947-1954
Miss Carla Holtermann	1947-1951
Miss Mary Winston	1948-1952
The Rev. Leon Zahn	1950-1953
Miss Eleanor Magnusson	1952-1955
Dr. Otto H. Dagefoerde	1951-1960
Mr. George Black	1956-1958
Mrs. Marjorie P. Carpenter	1956-1966
Miss Cornelia Wallace	1959-1964
Mr. Albert J. Olsen	1960-1966

**Immigration (Resettlement, Refugee) Service
Director**

Dr. Cordelia Cox	1949-1957
Mr. Vernon Bergstrom	1958-1961
Mr. Donald Anderson	1962-1966

**Clinical Pastoral Education
Secretary**

Dr. Henry H. Cassler	1962-1966

MILITARY PERSONNEL

(Service Commission 1941-1947; Bureau of Service 1948-1963; Division of Service 1964-1966)

Executive Secretaries

Dr. N. M. Ylvisaker	1941-1947
Dr. Gynther Storaasli	1949-1954
The Rev. Engebret O. Midboe	1954-1966
Dr. Carl F. Yaeger	1951-1964

Assistant Executive Secretary

The Rev. Herman E. Knies	1957-1966

AMERICAN MISSIONS

(Commission 1942-1943; Division 1944-1966)

Executive Secretary

Dr. N. Conrad Hoyer	1942-1960
Dr. Robert W. Long	1960-1966

Assistants to Executive Secretary

(Town & Country)	Dr. E. W. Mueller	1946-1966
(Urban Planning)	The Rev. C. P. Rasmussen	1950-1953
	Dr. Walter Kloetzli, Jr.	1954-1966
(Intercultural Outreach;	The Rev. Alf M. Kraabel	1956-1959
Human Relations)	The Rev. Lawrence W. Halvorson	1960-1964

Christian Approach to Jewish People
Secretary

Dr. Harold Floreen	1949-1952
The Rev. Nels Bergstrom	1953-1956

Ministry to Negro Communities
Secretary

The Rev. E. E. Krebs	1951-1954

COLLEGE AND UNIVERSITY WORK
(Commission on Student Service 1945-1948; Division of Student Service 1949-1955; Division of College and University Work 1956-1966)

Executive Secretary

Dr. Morris Wee	1946-1950
Dr. Donald Heiges	1951-1958
Dr. A. Henry Hetland	1959-1966

Assistant Executive Secretary

Dr. Ruth C. Wick	1947-1950
The Rev. Robert Larson	1954-1957
The Rev. Otto A. Bremer	1958-1962
Dr. Roy Enquist	1962-1965
(Finance)	
Mr. Kenneth Wester	1962-1966

Regional Directors

The Rev. Oswald Elbert	1947-1957
The Rev. Paul E. Bierstedt	1947-1960
Miss Norma Arneson	1950-1951
The Rev. Clyde Grimstvedt	1952-1953
Dr. A. Henry Hetland	1953-1958
The Rev. Earl T. Knaus	1957-1961
The Rev. Donald Hetzler	1960-1966
The Rev. John W. Arthur	1960-1966
The Rev. Gilbert Doan	1961-1965
The Rev. Kenneth C. Larson	1962-1966
The Rev. Albert Dillemuth	1962-1966
The Rev. Donald W. Herb	1962-1966

LUTHERAN WORLD FEDERATION AFFAIRS
(including USA Committee 1947-1966, Division of LWF Affairs 1956-1966)
European Desk
Secretary

Dr. John A. Scherzer	1949-1953

Executive Secretary: DLWFA
Dr. Stewart W. Herman   1956-1963

Latin America (Commission on L.A., 1951; Division 1951-1956; Department of Cooperation in L.A., 1956-1966)
Secretary
Dr. Stewart W. Herman   1951-1956

World Missions (Commission on Orphaned Missions 1948-1949; Commission on Orphaned Missions and Younger Churches 1949-1956; Department of World Missions Cooperation 1956-1966)
Secretary

Dr. Fredrik A. Schiotz	1948-1954
Dr. George F. Hall	1954-1956
The Rev. Oscar R. Rolander	1957-1961
The Rev. Donald E. Trued	1962-1966

Department of World Service
Secretary
Mr. Bernard A. Confer   1956-1966

Department of Theological Cooperation
Secretary

The Rev. Charles P. Carroll	1956-1958
Dr. David Granskou	1959-1963
Dr. Virgil Westlund	1963-1966

International Exchange Program
Secretary
Dr. Ruth C. Wick   1957-1966

LUTHERAN WORLD RELIEF
(agency closely related to NLC)
Executive Secretary
Mr. Bernard A. Confer   1946-1966

Assistant Executive Secretary
The Rev. Ove R. Nilesen   1956-1966

Administrative Secretary

Mr. Carl Lorey	1948-1961
Mr. Arthur Johnson	1962-1966

Overseas Commissioners

National Lutheran Council
Appointed by NLC—1919-1929

Dr. C. Theodore Benze	1923-1924
The Rev. A. C. Ernst	1922
The Rev. G. A. Fandrey	1919
Dr. Lauritz Larsen	1920, 1922
Dr. O. C. Mees	1925
Dr. George Rygh	1919
The Rev. W. L. Scheding	1922-1923
The Rev. H. J. Schuh	1919
Prof. M. J. Stolee	1920
Dr. S. G. Youngert	1919
Dr. J. A. Morehead	1919-1929
(Chairman)	

Appointed by NLC acting as USA Committee of LWF, or by

NLC Commission on Younger Churches and Orphaned Missions.*

Miss Edith Banuski	1951-1953
Dr. I. J. Bella	1947-1952
Dr. Nils Arne Bendtz	1952
Dr. Julius Bodensieck	1950-1953
The Rev. J. H. Deutschlander	1951
Dr. Martin Dietrich	1947-1952
The Rev. Philip Hoh	1951-1953
Dr. Howard Hong	1947-1949
Dr. Paul Lindberg	1949-1950
Dr. Carl Lund-Quist	1952
The Rev. Carl H. Mau, Jr.	1950-1953
Dr. Edwin Moll	1947-1952
Dr. Daniel Nelson	1947-1948
The Rev. Arthur S. Olson	1948-1952
Dr. David Ostergren	1948-1951
The Rev. Carl F. Schaffnit	1947-1948
Dr. John Schmidt	1951-1953

------

*Not included are representatives of the American Section of the Lutheran World Convention (1943-1947), of LWR unless jointly sponsored by U.S.A. Committee, or of LWF after 1952. Several of the men listed served earlier under the American Section, LWC, or later under the LWF.

Index

213